Memoirs of a London boy

In the 50's and 60's

(A hilarious and true look at poverty, survival
and life when things were so much simpler and
the kids happier)

By

Keith Coleman-Cooke

I would like to dedicate this book to my rather dysfunctional family for the humour of our childhood and the many laughs that we have had since then

I would also like to dedicate this book to my lovely wife Kathleen for her support in all that I attempt and to my two sons, Steven and Glenn, who have endured these stories over many years.

Contents

Introduction

After telling my younger son yet another story from my childhood my wife suggested that I write it all down in a book about growing up in the 50's and 60's. Yes, it would show that we were rather poor and many of the tricks and ducking and diving were designed to survive, which we did.

This is a book about poverty and deprivation but we did not see it like that at the time but it is a book about humour and how we saw ourselves both then and now.

I suppose this story must start before I was born and show some of the hardships that most people went through during and immediately after the Second World War.

Like many other people my mother was "bombed out" during the war and the only way they could survive was to squat in a property or rent something very cheap. When the war was over finding somewhere to live was very difficult and you took whatever was available.

This book is not about age related stories or a biography from A to Z. It is a collection of stories and anecdotes but not in any order, which I suppose sums up my life.

I have put together events as I remember them and to be honest, I also relied on members of my family for their interpretation of events. I have put the stories into chapters for ease of reference but as I said, they are not in any order or dates.

Times were very hard for most people in the early 50's. The war had finished in 1945 and the National Health Service did not start till 1948. There was still rationing and loads of damaged buildings that were known as bomb sites and that was where we often played as children, even though our parents had told us how dangerous they were (we always listen to our parents, right!)

There was very little, if any, political correctness or health and safety regulations and the children stayed out all day at the week-ends and during the school holidays, coming home when they were hungry or when the street lights came on. We peed behind a bush and shared water with loads of other kids from the same bottle.

Chapter One - Early Years

I was born in what my mother always referred to as "the wooden cottage" (more of that later) in Southend Lane, Sydenham, South London. After being bombed out of the place in Charlton before I was born and for those of you old enough to remember, Southend Lane was the road down the side of Peter Pans Pool which was a permanent children's play site with a few rides and a boating pool. As a special treat, we would be allowed to go on the boats or on the rides which we thought was great.

Unfortunately, it has long since gone, to be replaced by yet another supermarket. But after a couple of years I then went with the family to a homeless families' hostel in Plumstead, South London and it was called "a rest centre". Now don't ask me why, as according to mother, nobody got very much rest !! Only the women and children could stay there. The men had to fend for themselves but apparently, most men, my father included, would visit in the early evening, leave by the front door at the allotted time and just as quickly go round the back and come in through the window to stay the night!

We all lived in the one room and opposite our room was the shared kitchen where each family would cook their meals and then take the food back to the one room to eat. Now apparently, there was a sort of eating area upstairs but most families preferred to eat in their room.

Whilst we were living at the hostel two of my elder brothers, Terry and Bud were out playing when they found a bomb. Yes, you did get that right, it was a live bomb but to be fair to them they thought that it was an empty shell. They were rolling it down the hill and throwing it around between their mates when a man saw them and nearly had a heart attack, as he recognised it as a live shell. He called the police and the army bomb disposal unit came and made it safe.

It was from the hostel that we were re-housed to a 3 bedroom flat at Ballamore Road on the Downham estate on the border of South London and Kent and it is from here that I suppose the story really starts,

The Downham estate was built in the 1930's, as London was expanding and there was a shortage of council housing. Remember that back in the 50's and 60's there were 2 sources of council housing; first there was Lewisham Borough Council and then there was the London County Council, who would also have the responsibility of putting toilet paper in public toilets. On each sheet there was printed the initials 'LCC'! Of course if we managed to nick one from a public toilet then anyone using our toilet at home would be told that we were a bit posh. as Terry's real name was Len Colin Cooke or LCC !!!

There were a minimum of 8 people living in that flat but to be honest there always seemed to be a lot more than that as during the war Mum had managed to pick up a couple of "extras" in the form of two boys called Colin and John.

Both boys had lost their parents in an air raid and were left homeless and mum did not think they should be in an orphanage. In those days there was no such thing as fostering, so she decided to take them in and look after them until they were old enough to go out into the big wide world.

Colin never lived with us at Ballamore as he had long since left our nest and he went on to become an air traffic controller, first at Croydon Airport and then at Heathrow. He got married and carried on living in the Croydon area.

John stayed with us a bit longer and he after left school he got a job at a local bike shop where he stayed until he joined the Royal Marines.

There was often the odd uncle (e.g. friends of my father) who always seemed to "lodge" with us.

The family breakdown is rather difficult to follow so pay attention and try not to fall asleep, ok!

There was Dad, whose name was Dean but he was known as Danny. There was Mum whose name was Agnes, but everyone knew her as Rose except for the loads of nieces and nephews who knew her as Aunt Aggie. Mum was one of thirteen children, are you still following this??

My eldest brother is called Albert and that is what we had to call him but at work he was always known as Bert, but if any of his siblings had called him that he would have hit the roof.

The next one down was christened Peter Arthur Lawrence and his Initials spelt PAL and according to one of Mum's American friends, (no, don't ask) a PAL is a Buddy and he has been known as that ever since! Although now that he is a grown up we call him Bud.

I do hope that you are following this as it gets a bit more complicated as we go on!

The next in line was Terry (now sadly deceased) who we think was actually Christened Derek, although nobody is very sure as I think you can understand why. All the relatives called him 'Terry the Terror' but was always known as Tel.

Terry was only young, maybe 5 or 6 when he disappeared for a whole day. Friends, neighbours and the police were involved in the search for him. When he turned up later in the day and was asked where he had been, he said he had been to the cemetery on a "borrowed" tricycle. There were some graves that had lots of flowers and some that had none, so he shared them out so that all the graves had some flowers. Everyone thought that was so nice although I suspect that the owners of the flowers were not that impressed!

Next in line comes little me, Keith, and with this comes a little confusion. I was always led to believe that it was my cousin Lena who gave me the nickname *Keefy Doos* but some members of the family seem to think that is was another cousin called Maureen. However, this manifested itself into *Doosy* (not to be confused with dozy and has remained with some members of the family ever since.

The last but by no means least is my sister Pamela who was Christened Pamela Deanna (any idea where that came from?) Rose. As a small child, she had very fair, curly hair which looked like bubbles and that is why she became known as Bubbles by all the family but most of us now refer to her as Bubs.

I was born Keith Dean (there appears to be a trend here!) Cooke on 13th November 1947 in what my mother called "the wooden cottage" in Sydenham, South London. I remember stories of that "cottage" as it had an outside toilet and no running water so therefore no washing or bathing facilities. To all extents and purposes, it was a bit rough but always referred to as the "cottage". The family would have to use the public baths just around the corner, but not me as I was just a baby!

Now, to get the next bit into perspective, my wife and I sold a business in 1998 and moved into a large detached house with a tennis court, swimming pool and a garden of nearly an acre in size. The hallway was larger than the flat we lived in when we first got married!

In about 2004 my Uncle Len came to visit and as soon as he entered the hallway he said "oh very nice, not bad for a boy born in a hovel" Now Uncle Len was in his eighties then and, never one to mince his words, when we started talking about where I was born and I referred to the "cottage", Uncle Len started to laugh, "Cottage? cottage?, it was a f***ing shed!". Oh well, another myth put to bed, but at least me and Jesus had something in common, we were both born in a shed!!!

In the process of writing this book I have found out a bit more about "the cottage". They were in fact a row of small wooden cottages that were condemned, they had no glass in the windows and my two oldest brothers, Albert and Bud, hung material over the window frames to keep out the cold. They did this every night and the next morning had to remove some or all of the so-called curtains.

Albert and Bud both remember doing this, but of course I was too young. The place had no running water (they collected water in a bucket from Uncle Len and Aunt Wins' flat just around the corner) and it also had an outdoor toilet, but I assume that it was a question of 'needs must'.

I am not sure how long we stayed at the cottage before being placed in the homeless families' hostel, but before we moved out, my eldest brother Albert moved in with Aunt Win and Uncle Len and stayed with them for some time.

It was Uncle Len that taught Albert many of life's 'do's and don'ts' - such as never tuck your shirt into your underpants as you then get shit on your shirt tails and when you take your shirt off when changing for football, all the other kids would take the micky if they could see the shit. But they could not see inside your underpants and thus could not see any shit and therefore not take the micky! What a clever man Uncle Len was!!

We moved into our flat in about 1951 when I was about four years of age. My mother thought it was great, as for the first time, she had an inside bathroom. But I do tell people that we had an outside toilet in the flat and it was true. You had to go out on the balcony to gain access to the toilet, and in the winter, it was freezing cold and not the sort of place that where you wanted to linger.

I went to the local primary school called Ballamore Road Infants and my earliest memories are of the camp beds, which came out after lunch and all the reception class children had to have a sleep for about an hour, long enough for the staff to get in the staff room for coffee and fags!!

Another memory from that time was standing outside the school with my Mum waving goodbye to my older brother as he went on a coach to see the coronation. I do remember crying, as I was deemed to be too young to go, but the good news was that there was only one family in our road who had a television and they very kindly invited most of the street into their front room to see the ceremony. I do remember it was packed with all the children sitting on the floor at the front, then adults on chairs and then adults standing at the back.

My one other lasting memory of my primary school was the "Rose Queen" ceremony where the Rose Queen marries her prince. Some schools called this the May Queen Ceremony as this was the event where some of the children danced around the May Pole. Now they always picked the blond haired, blue eyed good looking kids for those two roles. The other leading role was the vicar who marries them. This child had to be able to read and be rather loud and the only one to meet this criterion was the ugly kid with big ears and glasses, not a blond blue eyed child that they wanted! Yes, you got it, me, which I think upset some of the teachers! Someone in the family still has a photo of me as the vicar in the Rose Queen ceremony.

Also around that time most of the kids around our estate had "nits" which in those days were not easy to eradicate (nice word that), so the NHS appointed a "Nit Nurse". Of course, this was not just our estate but all areas of London and possibly beyond. Most families felt a little ashamed if the Nit Nurse visited them and found that the children had nits. So, when she was spotted doing her rounds, the word would go out that "Nitty Nora" was about and not to answer your door or, to make out you were out so when others asked if "Nitty Nora" had been to your house, you could honestly answer "No"!

My Dad was Irish (we think, as we cannot find any birth records) and liked a drink; in fact, he liked a few drinks and when drunk anything could happen and often did.

I must have been about 9 years old when a friend of mine knocked on our door and said he had been sent by his mum to ask if we would go and collect our Dad who was crashed out, drunk in their front garden. I don't know why, but they found this rather disconcerting. Luckily both Albert and Bud were home as they had the muscle to get him. This was not an unusual occurrence, although to be fair, most times he managed to stagger home under his own steam, with only the occasional foray into neighbours' gardens.

Chapter Two - Scrumping & Scams

My Mum was not all sweetness and light and on many occasions, could be very volatile to Dad, the lodgers, the neighbours, burglars and the kids.

My brother Albert, his wife Jean and their children lived with us twice. The first time was in 1954 when my father was alive and it was a planned move into our flat. To make them feel at home, Mum got their son a black and white beach ball to play with but, much to the disgust of both my sister and myself, we were not allowed to play with it. Also, as part of the "welcome to the flat" Mum had made a special effort by using a tablecloth made from old newspapers; you see, we were posh!! They left the first time in about 1957 to live in Hither Green and the second time they lived with us must have been about 1960 and they stayed with us until they got their council house in 1963.

We did have certain standards which we had to adhere to; for instance, nobody could wear hats in the flat (that included children and adults) and if we had been in the garden with our shirts off, then you were not allowed at the meal table until you put your shirt back on.

The other very strict rule was "no elbows on the table". Now again, this applied to both adults and children but sometimes, while waiting for our food to be dished up, we would rest our head on our hand which meant our elbow was on the table and if my father (or after his death, my eldest brother) saw this they would come along and knock your elbow off the table, which very often meant that your head smacked onto the table. Not a great experience and it hurt like bloody hell.

Another reality check was that we did not have carpets in the flat. We had lino which Mum kept in immaculate condition. The bloody stuff was very shiny and very slippery so if you ran around in your socks, then you could well end up on your arse sliding towards the radio. I also remember when we got a very large rug which sat in the middle of the living room and was warm and comfy to walk on, but the dangerous bit was if you ran across the rug and did not stop before reaching the lino, again, you could kiss your arse goodbye.

I also remember having a mat in our bedroom which I always thought was strange as the boys had a gazunder (this is a potty that 'gazunder' the bed). Even if boys are wide awake, they very often can miss so half asleep and trying to pee into a gazunder, could very often leave all areas on and around the mat rather soggy. Now if my brother got up first, and I had missed, he would not be very happy.

Sometimes when dad came home drunk and started a row, (you know where this is going!!) and yes you are right, the gazunder went over Dad's head and at this point I should think Mum told him to piss off!

Very soon after they came to live with us for the first time, Jean won a very nice embroidered fire guard at the works raffle which took pride of place in front of the open fire when not alight. Dad was a little worse for wear one day and started a row with Mum, (never a great idea) which ended when Mum picked up the lovely fire guard and smashed it over Dad's head. That put an end to both the argument and the fire guard and my sister-in-law Jean still talks about it to this day.

Most of our family worked at the same engineering factory in Hither Green at one time or another. When I was young, about seven or eight, we went to a Christmas party at the factory and as was a great tradition Father Christmas was there to give us all presents. But I think the dick head, who had labelled the presents, had done so in age only and not by age and gender, so I got this rather large doll, which to be honest, I hated it and burst into tears.

Now luckily there was a little girl sat nearby also in tears as she did not like the idea of twin cowboy guns and holsters, so peace prevailed as the two mums got together when they realised that they both had the same problem and we happily swopped the doll for the cowboy guns. Another result!!

Before they came to live with us the first time we had no TV, so of a weekend Albert would load his TV into a pram and they would come for the week-end so that we could at least see some television.

Dad had a variety of jobs. On my birth certificate, it showed that he worked as a factory labourer. He had his own ice cream franchise, *D Cooke Fine Ices* and a bike with a cold box on the front. The family still has photos and I remember going to the shop where he got his ice creams from in Catford. But Dad was a bit of a rascal and I remember being told that he had won £200 on the football pools, which was great! We got a new rug for the living room and we all got some new clothes. Very soon after that "win" Dad went up to Chesterfield for a while and it was only when I was in my 40's that I found out that Dad had nicked the takings from the ice cream shop and then did a runner to Chesterfield but at least we kept the rug and the clothes.

Dad was a sort of pseudo Christian who was thinking about becoming a Catholic priest when war broke out but joined the RAF in the stores. Yes, yes, you do know what is coming and yes, my Mum and elder brothers did have jam and jellies throughout the war. My eldest brother remembers knocks on the door in the middle of the night asking, *"Is your name Rose"* and when he got a positive answer, he would then say that *"Danny has sent this for you"*. There were all sorts of rationed foodstuff in the boxes and of course there was also the much sought after parachute silk, which was used to make underwear for mother and I suspect some of her sisters as well.

After the war, Dad became a Methodist lay preacher. Now this was a little difficult because at the time Methodists were not supposed to drink or smoke, which for a smoking, pissed Irishman should have posed some problems, but he seemed to get away with it, as he did many things including holding a raffle for a fine Irish linen table cloth and napkins. The proceeds of the raffle were meant for the church and everyone in the street seemed to buy tickets, but I suspect that the person who won it was the owner anyway and the pair of them split the takings.

Life was ok at this time when Dad was working. He told everyone he worked for the Admiralty, which in fact was the truth, however he made it sound like he was the First Lord of the Admiralty when in fact he was a stoker in the boiler room. But one of the better parts of Dads work was that every year the admiralty had a families' sports day with loads of great prizes and even if you came last, as I did on one occasion when I had just come out of hospital, you got a very good prize.

One year we were held up and were a bit late arriving at the park in Wimbledon and caught a taxi from the station with my brother Bud changing into his running gear in the taxi. Now when I say 'running gear' I mean an old vest, a pair of school gym shorts and a pair of plimsolls and when he arrived at the start line there were a few sniggers from some of the other lads in their posh gear and spikes. Well, Bud ran that 100 yards (not metres then) like the wind and well beat the rest, so the scruffy poor kid struck a blow. Yes, well done Bud! I also ran the 100 yards but as I said above, I had not long been out of hospital and I think I had only had the stitches removed a day or two before, so I ended up taking about 5 minutes to run the race. I can still do that same time today! I do remember getting a huge cheer from the crowd and a great prize but I can't remember what it was!!

All our social life at this time was dictated by church activities and on a Sunday, we would all go as a family to the 10.00 service. We would then go home for Sunday lunch and the children would go back at 14.00 for Sunday school. Sometimes we were also known to go to the evening service, although this was not every week.

Dad was in the operatic society, yes he did have a good voice, and he was also in the drama society. I remember going to see him perform on stage in the church hall, and whatever play it was, he played the role of a postman. The same hall also showed films and one we watched was about a troop of boys being lost in the jungle, which must have had a profound effect on me as I still remember it about 60 years on.

Dad had 2 brothers who he did not speak to or have any contact with for many years. In 1978, twenty years after my father died, one of his brothers made contact with us and he told me that back in the 50's he rode his bike from London to Reading to hear Dad sing at a large theatre. As they were still not talking, he stayed up in the gods (the cheap seats at the top of the theatre) where Dad could not see him, but he could still see and hear Dad sing.

My elder brothers were in the Boys Club and my brother Terry was a very good gymnast, although we could not afford to go and watch him. He was part of a gymnastic display created by the London Boy's Clubs at the Royal Albert Hall and I think Mum went along to see him.

Another of Terry's rather odd hobbies was that he was involved with a bloke from the church who apparently was a photographer for a modelling agency and ask mother if he could take some photos of Terry. I must admit I could see why as he was a fair haired, slim, good looking lad aged about ten years old. Mother agreed Terry and went to either his house or a room at the church (yes, I know you can see where this is going) and he then took some photos of Terry which were ok. I think Mum rather liked them but things went wrong when Terry came home from one session with copies of last week's photos which showed Terry in a very skimpy swimming costume and nothing else!!

Now that got Mother thinking that this did not seem right and so she decided that this should stop, as anyone taking photos of a 10-year-old in skimpy underwear or swimming costume must be very suspect. Although I am not sure if Dad ever got involved or even gave an opinion, but as far as I know, the bloke continued going to church, maybe to look for other vulnerable children.

The first organised sort of club that I joined was the "Cubs" who met in a church hall just across the road from our flat. The reason I wanted to join was because they often passed our flat on the way to their meetings and I not only loved the look of their uniform, but they also seemed to be having great fun. Whenever they played games on the grass outside the church hall, I started to attend but unfortunately it only lasted for about 2 to 3 weeks before I was thrown out for being disruptive, which was a shame. But then again, Dad thought that I should go to something at his church and to that end I joined the Life Boys, which were the part of the boys brigade for younger lads. We went to Life Boys every week, plus of course there were various "Parade" days such as Remembrance Sunday.

There were about 3 or 4 of us that used to go from our end of town. We would be given sixpence or 6d as it was then; 1 penny (1d) each way on the bus, 1d subs and 3d for a bag of chips on the way home. But one day we were devastated when Mr L, the chip shop owner, told us that he had put the chips up to 4d, but said that we could always have them for 3d if we were in uniform.

If we had fish and chips it would always be from Mr L's in Grove Park and we would also get tuppence worth (2d) of Crackling, no not pork crackling, but the odd bits that fall off the batter during cooking and when we got home they would be shared out to the adults as most of the kids did not like them anyway.

As I was a rather sickly and skinny child someone in the family had the great idea that it would do me the world of good to toughen up a bit and to that end I was encouraged to go with a mate to the local boxing club. This was not a good idea from the start as I am allergic to physical violence and to be honest, I was not looking forward to some kid smacking me in the face. But having said all that, I do remember getting to the semi-final of a competition held at Lewisham Town Hall in Catford and Mum came to watch, so I could not have been that bad. But I do think that it was soon after that when I decided getting beaten up for a hobby was not for me.

For a fair amount of time in my childhood I used to grow vegetables in our garden and I would often get advice and encouragement from both Mr W upstairs or Mr J who lived next door to the flats.

The one thing that I remember I was very successful at growing were Radishes, but they were so good and so hot that neither me or anyone else could eat them and yet the Radishes of today lack not only any flavour but also that lovely "Bite" associated with the old-fashioned Radish. I also remember growing some spuds which were also a minor success as we could all eat them!! Mr W would always refer to me as 'Farmer Giles', God knows who he was??

Our garden was not huge, but it did have a massive Oak tree, which was great for kids to climb and fall out of but there was also an old Anderson shelter in our neighbour's garden. This was at the end of the row of gardens and I assume the reason they built it there was because it was the furthest point away from the building itself therefore giving the residents some chance to survive if they were in the shelter and the flats took a direct hit. If you remember them then I am sure you must have a smile on your face but for those of you who do not know what the hell we are talking about then I will explain. An Anderson shelter was made of corrugated iron which was placed in a hole in the ground and covered with earth and would at least give you a little protection if a bomb fell nearby.

As there was not a lot of money around Dad sometimes bought a bag of sweets to share out, although with the amount of people in our flat you never got many sweets. We would find ways of earning money and one of the ways would be to go around the houses with an old pram and collect any old newspapers and then take them to Mr L at the chip shop in Grove Park, who would give us a little money which would often be spent on sweets.

Oh, they did seem to be a lot bigger and a lot nicer, such as the Wagon Wheels. I swear they have shrunk over the years or it maybe it is that we were little and they just looked bigger!!

I can still remember many of the sweets we used to buy and some of course are still available today, such as Flying Saucers, which I still get from time to time, but only when the grandchildren are not staying!

How about liquorice sticks, which were just like pieces of wood that you would get from a tree. You did not really eat them as much as suck all the liquorice from the stick. Wow they were lovely, as were sherbet dips. Do you remember how they made your eyes water? Gobstoppers kept you quiet for some time and were much loved by parents, as well as Jamboree bags that contained a variety of little sweets.

Of course, in those days the shops were all local shops with no supermarkets, but later a small Co-Op opened at Grove Park and I remember that the co-op gave 'divi's' (dividends) in the form of tin coins. Come on, who remembers them? Every time you bought anything at the Co-Op you had to give your "Co-Op dividend number" which I must admit I had long since forgotten. But to my utter surprise, my sister still remembers the number and when she told me it was 105576, it all came flooding back.

The owners of all the other shops were in the main local people, who were part of the local community so if they caught anyone shoplifting, the shop keeper would not go to the police but would report the offender to a fate worse than death. His mother!!

Another way that we managed to "earn" a few bob was to climb the fence behind the local off-licence, which was part of the pub in those days, and take a few lemonade bottles, go around to the front and return the bottle to the landlord who would then give you a penny on each bottle returned. In other words; he would return your 'deposit'! Wow, it took him a long time to understand that they were his bottles he was buying back. When he did realise what we were doing, we would still take the bottles, but took them to another off licence or shop until they all realised that they were being conned and started to stamp the labels with some sort of logo.

It was outside of this pub that Mum witnessed a fight between an Italian and a local man who were giving it very large when the Italian man started to shout "Bastardo, Bastardo" which made the local man more annoyed. He said "stop calling me a bastard and I will stop hitting you" to which the Italian replied "Bastardo, Bastardo". Oh well, maybe the local man went on holiday to Italy many years later and learnt that Bastardo means 'enough'!

There were other ways to earn money depending on the time of year, for instance, "Penny for the guy" was always a good little earner depending on where your pitch was. October half term is the perfect time to collect as you could stay out by the station all day and earn a few quid over the course of a couple of weeks. Friday evening was also a very lucrative time to collect being payday.

Remember that we had never heard of Halloween at that time so there was no Trick or Treating and I believe that it was not until the 70's that the children started Trick or Treating.

Carol singing could also be a good earner if you thought about it and organised yourselves! If you had a friend who could play the recorder, that would help and if you had a very young brother or sister then people felt sorry for you and gave a bit more. But to be honest the only one who could sing a bit was my brother Tel, who had a decent voice and if we listened to Tel, he would help to keep us all in tune or very nearly in tune. As he was the good looking one, being at the front also helped.

Another scam we used if we were skint was to go to the sidings at our Local railway station where the coal wagons would dump their loads until trucks came and picked up the coal to be distributed to coal merchants. We would go down the side of the fence, which was like the fencing you get on tennis courts, and if you lifted the bottom and kick the fence, a fair bit of coal fell out, as would the Nutty Slack, which is what my mother called the coal dust. Now this coal dust had a very important role to play as did potato skins?? Let me explain.

We would load the coal into the pram and get it home as quickly as possible to avoid getting caught as in those days there always seemed to be a copper about and they knew most people on their patch and would keep a very close eye on some members of the community e.g. our family and friends, to ensure that you were keeping to the right side of the law but in a very cold winter I am sure that he turned a blind eye so that we could at least have some heat but of course when we got home we looked like we had been up someone's chimney and it would take ages stood by the sink to get the coal dust off but at least while we were doing that the flat was warm.

In the very cold winter when we had the coal fire going, just before bedtime Mother would put a little coal on the fire, followed by loads of potato peelings and all covered with the nutty slack. Then in the morning you gave it a good rake around with the poker and the fire would spring back to life and start warming the flat immediately without having to wait ages for the fire to get going first.

The local bobby would also try to catch us scrumping, which he did not do very well except for one time when he caught me and gave me a clip round the ear. It bloody hurt and when I got home I had to tell my Mother that one of my mates had done it when messing about. And yes, it was a coincidence that I also had some "windfalls" which, unbeknown to Mum, the local bobby had let me keep as he would have had to get rid of them somehow, so it was easier for him to let us keep them.

Another of our little scams, and a way to get coal, was to follow the coalman when he made his deliveries. He would pull a large sack of coal to the edge of the lorry and then haul it onto his shoulders and of course a few lumps of coal would fall into the road.

While the coalman was in the house we would very quickly run over, pick up the coal and disappear again before he came out of the house. It was great to hide and see his face as he was looking for the coal which he knew he had dropped. He also knew when we were about but he would not leave his lorry to come and look for us as, while he was away from his lorry, a lot more coal may have gone missing.

Food was often in short supply so anything to supplement the budget was a winner, Mum constantly told us that scrumping was stealing but collecting wind falls, for example apples that had fallen to the ground, was ok and legal (not so sure about that but who were we to argue).So in the season we would go to certain places collecting windfalls - ok, so we told fibs!

On one occasion my brother Tel, Bubs and I went scrumping; remembering that Bubs is three years younger than me so Bubs was about six and I must have been about nine, which made Tel twelve. This farmer was known to fire his shotgun at people scrumping his fruit and we could handle that (is that why I joined the Army?), but we did not know that he had an Alsatian dog that was grumpier than his owner.

Now, have you tried running with your shirt full of apples and a bloody big dog growling and closing in on your arse? Brotherly love and the need to protect your little sister has now been blown away and it comes down to the survival of the fittest or fastest and unfortunately Bubs was neither. So when we got to the stream both Tel and I leapt across and hoped that the dog would not follow. As it happened, the dog did not want to follow us as he had found that Bubs was not as fast as us and decided that he would embed his teeth in her arse instead. This focused her mind and she got across the stream but I think that Tel and I were grounded while Bubs recovered from her dog bite. I must say at this point that, for the past 50 plus years she has been willing to show off her scar to anyone who had the courage to look!

I do remember that there always seemed to be loads of people living in the flat at any one time. There was my eldest brother Albert and his wife Jean, plus their three children in one bedroom the second time they came to live with us. Mum and Bubs were in the second bedroom and in the third bedroom were Bud, Terry and myself. Then there was a bed in the living room for Uncle Fred.

There was also a friend of Bud's called Wally who had been thrown out by his parents when he broke his leg in a motorbike accident and he was crashing out on our settee. Wally used to have fits and I remember him having a fit in the living room, so you can see that there would have been severe logistical problems with twelve of us living in a three-bedroomed flat.

Remember that we did not have such a thing as duvets in those days. I never saw one until the late 1960's and that was in a hotel in Germany and I was a little bit suspicious of that new-fangled thing.

We only had sheets and a blanket and as we had no heating in the bedrooms, in the winter if it was very cold we would put overcoats on top of the blanket to try and keep warm. It did not always work.

Chapter Three - Food & Violence

Fridays were always pay day and therefore shopping day. We would take the old pram, yes, the same one that the coal went in, and head to the shop in Downham Way as they were better than our closest local shops. Do remember that most of the time there were over twelve people in that flat so there was a lot of food. For instance Mum would buy 2 x 28lb bags of potatoes and they would lay under the main bodywork of the pram on a flimsy rack and all the other shopping would go inside the pram. Our last port of call was the butchers shop where we would get our meat for the week. There were no sell by dates then and you could buy your week's meat in one go.

Now do remember that in those days we did not have a fridge; all we had was a larder cupboard with a marble slab which kept food cool. The rules were simple, you checked to see if it looked ok, you then smelt it and if it also smelt ok then you cooked it. As there were no sell by or use by dates on any food, it was left up to you to decide if you wished to poison your family or not!

We would also get peas pudding (the yellow stuff and not green as they have "up North") and faggots for our tea. I still love faggots to this day, although we can only buy frozen ones now but in those days the local butchers all made their own. They would be double wrapped in newspaper and put in the middle of the shopping to keep warm until we got home. If we timed it right we, could get the shopping unloaded, up the stairs, put away and have our peas pudding and fagots ready to eat just as "Journey into space" started on the radio.

Some things, such as the above ritual were etched in stone, they did not change and only fire or flood could affect it, such was the Sunday bath ready for school or work the following day and do bare in mind that we only had the one bath a week, we did not have running hot water but we did have a dirty great boiler at theend of the bath that was a bit like a 45 gallon drum sat on a gas ring with a pipe that dropped down into the bath thus filling it with hot water.

Now as you can imagine, when there are twelve or more people needing baths we could not afford to pay for the gas to keep the boiler going all evening. So each bath would have a very small amount of hot water added to a large amount of cold water, thus giving everyone a tepid bath. Now that was not very pleasant but it gets worse! The way to have more hotter water was for everyone to share. So, this was how it went: Mum and girls had a bath in fresh water and then fresh water for men and boys. But being the youngest boy, and the fact that all lodgers and any other uncles or hangers on were of the male gender came before me, this left me having a bath in the Ganges. In fact, I am sure that sometimes I emerged with clods of earth all over my body and on many occasions, I swear that I came out of the bath dirtier than when I went in! Of course, being the last one to have a bath, it was stone bloody cold anyway!

There was not a lot of room in the bathroom and I use that term very loosely. The bath was about 30 inches wide and maybe there was another 2 feet in which to get dressed or undressed and the boiler was at the foot of the bath. Now some people are more agile than others; for instance skinny little me had no problems in such a small space, but Bubs, who had the uncanny ability to be able to break a plate by just looking at it, found bath nights very difficult. Then one night we heard screaming from the bathroom, but as all the boys were banished from the area, we only found out later that when she bent down to put on her knickers, she pressed her arse against the very hot boiler! You can see a pattern emerging here can't you! First the dog bite and now the boiler; her arse must look like a map of the Western desert during the war, all pot holes!

As you can imagine food played a very important role within the household. Yes, there were times when most of the cupboard was bare, and do remember we did not have a fridge, so the milk was kept in a bucket of water on the balcony and if it started to turn (go off) Mum would then boil it up for hot cocoa. Everything else was kept in the larder and the marble slab would keep the food cool and therefore last longer.

There were many times when the only thing in the larder was bread and dripping and even then Mum would often say "there is no bread so you will have to have toast"! Yes, we were a bit slow but in fact what she meant was that the bread was too stale to eat as a sandwich, or it was an odd shape because she had cut off the mouldy bits. As she did with most things like vegetables that were on the turn or the cheese, which she still did many years on. Come on, tell the truth, do you still cut off the mouldy bit on that last bit of cheese in the fridge or do you throw it out and do without your cheese sandwich?!!

We would have dripping on toast for breakfast. Now as it happens I still love a bit of beef dripping on toast but as there seems to be very little fat on the beef we have today in this healthy eating culture, you do not get as much and although I am sure that this is better for you, it does stop the likes of myself having a nice drop of dripping on toast and a possible heart attack!!

If the adults wanted to make a sandwich for work and we had some fresh bread and some that was stale, they would use one fresh slice and one stale slice to make their sandwich. These days that sounds horrific, I would prefer to have used the stale bread. I also have memories of mother pouring water over a stale loaf and then putting it in the oven to soften the inside and crisp up the outside and it would then smell and taste like a freshly baked loaf, but of course you had to eat it straight away or it would then go very hard again.

When I was a lad one of life's treats was a dirty great steak (stewing steak) and kidney suet pudding. Bearing in mind that in those days beef was the cheapest meat and chicken was very expensive. My mouth is watering as I write this! Mum would make it in a huge pudding bowl and then put the bowl inside a pillowcase (mine) and steam it for what felt like days with all the fantastic smells lingering in the air and we would ask dozens of times "is it ready yet" just like when going on a bloody day trip!

After the steak and kidney pudding was eaten, Mum would shake out the pillowcase and then put it on the boiler to dry and when it was dry it would go back on my bed. Now this was ok except that when I went to school the next day and any kids sat next to me, they would always start to feel hungry long before dinner time as they could smell the pudding in my hair. To this day, I still enjoy a steak and kidney pudding but of course nobody steams them any more as you can buy them to go into the microwave for just a few minutes. Not the same but I still enjoy them.

Sunday was always a good day for food as we would have roast beef and Yorkshire pudding which Mum cooked in a bloody great square oven dish and she would then cut it into squares for Sunday dinner. There would also be enough left over for the kids to have cold Yorkshire pudding with jam for tea complete with winkle sandwiches, oh, we knew how to live! Mum would always cook too many potatoes and greens. My eldest brother Albert would always have the green water to drink. I tried it once but found it disgusting but as far as I am aware he still drinks it to this day. Any vegetables left over would become bubble and squeak for Monday's tea together with the cold meat that was left over.

Sunday tea time was always the same. We would wait for the winkle man who would ring a large hand bell to let everyone know that he was there and Mum would get some shrimps for the adults and winkles for the children and there would be some salad stuff as well. If you have ever had the pleasure of getting a winkle out of its shell with a pin you will appreciate the size of the thing; it is tiny and looks even smaller because it is curled up. Now imagine making a sandwich out of just 4 winkles - it does not take a bloody genius to work out that it is all bloody bread and very little winkle. Mum would cut the sandwich into four squares with each square containing a winkle and then "utopia"! I left school and started work and I had agreed with Mum that I would contribute £1.10/- a week towards the housekeeping and as I was now a fully-fledged paying adult, I was then entitled to shrimps on a Sunday and as I was no longer a child, I did not get the winkles!!

Most days we had the same food: Sunday roast beef, Monday cold meat and bubble and squeak, Friday was peas pudding and fagots and Saturday was always mince and potatoes with fresh crusty bread. Try and imagine 1lb of mince being shared between about twelve people; it was all bloody gravy and very little meat. It was only in later years that I realised there was meat in it and I just thought that the gravy had bits in it. But I still enjoy it now. We would also have sausage and mash on one night which I loved and still do.

The whole family loved liver and bacon except little me. Now do remember in our house you were not made to eat anything, although at one time if you did not eat your dinner then it would be served up again at tea time. But this did not work very well because if my brothers thought that I did not want to eat it they would, so there was nothing left to give you for the next meal. So, Mum said that if you do not eat your meal you would get nothing else till the next meal time; no snacks or little nibbles if any were available.

Once when I was given liver and bacon I started to eat it and threw up all over the place, which did give Mother a bit of a clue that I didn't like it. She still tried it again and I still threw up so she decided that maybe it was a good idea not to give me liver and bacon. But when she cooked it for the rest of the family, I would smell it as soon as I entered the flats and by the time I got to our flat I was gagging and retching and would have to go on the balcony for a short time so I could then cope with the smell.

Many other dishes and food from my childhood that people no longer cook include suet pudding and bacon and onion roll. This was made with a very large flat piece of rolled out suet on which would then be laid bits of streaky bacon, this would be rolled over and then onions added and continued till either you ran out of bacon or you came to the end of the suet.

Stewed eels, which either myself or my brother Tel had caught and brought home, and, as Mum loved stewed eels, she would not ask where we had caught them. Whelks and stuffed hearts which I loved but I have not had for many years and it is only my older friends and family that remember them.

Black pudding eaten raw or fried in a sandwich with mustard (most of my family and friends turn their noses up at eating raw black pudding, but I love it) and of course every sort of pie you can imagine. Pigs' trotters and peas, and stuffed breast of lamb, which I have recently noticed in a supermarket, stuffed and ready to cook. All that has gone forever as there is no need to cook in this microwave society.

Mr B down the road was a postman so he started work very early but was also finished early. He used to go pigeon shooting in the afternoons and his wife would make pigeon pies. We would go scrumping for apples, pears and plums and Mum would make up the fruit into pies which we would exchange for pigeon pies. But of course, as children, we would not have eaten them if we had known they were pigeon so Mum told us they were chicken pies and we believed her. It was only as an adult in the army that I realised that chicken was very different from my childhood days. Also, remember that as we did not have a freezer, anything that was baked had to be eaten in 2 or 3 days so we could have pigeon pie and fruit pies coming out of our ears for a few days and then nothing for a while. But with the pigeons from Mr B and the rabbits from Albert we did not do too badly.

We would often shout up to Mum to ask what was for tea, "surprise pie" would be one reply or "bread and pullit", but the one that I remembered most was "pigs, sticks and onions" which I interpreted as pigs trotters and onions. It was only when I was in my 40's that my sister and elder brother informed me that she was in fact saying "pigs dicks and onions" now that changes it completely.

I could go on about food forever (yes, I know I have) because when I think of my childhood food was such a dominant feature that has stayed with me. The baker called every day with the bread on his cart and I remember when he stopped delivering we then had to walk round to the shops in Grove Park to get our bread but if you left it until late in the day you would get it cheaper as they could not sell it the next day. You could get yesterday's "stale" cakes very cheap, otherwise we would not have been able to afford cakes and in fact I can very clearly remember paying using some Farthings, who remembers them? I think it was something like 3d 3 farthings and for that we got a big bag of cakes, which equates to under 2p but of course price was relevant to earnings.

Later, in the early 60's my Mother used the local butchers a lot and that was because she got on very well with the manager, in fact so well that she ended up marrying him. A shrewd lady was mother, as she never went without meat again and I must admit that the quality of our meat did improve.

As a boy, I remember everything was delivered and most of them delivered by horse and cart. Our milkman was called Harry and I remember him from a very early age. Every morning he would come into our flat for a cup of tea and for Mum to learn all the local gossip.

Harry stayed our milkman right up until we left the area when we got a council house with a garden. It was on the same estate but out of Harry's area.

When my elder brothers helped Harry, mainly at Christmas when things got very busy, he was still using the horse and cart but by the time I helped him he had gone on to the milk float. He moaned most of the time about the float and about how he preferred the horse to all the modern technology. How would he cope today? But the other thing I remember most about helping Harry was that he would treat you to a full breakfast in the local café and I am sure that it was the first time that I had ever had a full English.

Others that came by horse and cart included the rag and bone man and he continued to come by horse and cart until we moved out of the area and he may have continued for many years.

Most of our crockery and cutlery came from the rag and bone man and if you played your cards right, at the end of a local jumble sale you could get a great big pile of clothes for a penny or two, but when the rag and bone man came you might get a couple of cups and a plate for that pile of clothes. So sometimes it was worth buying up the crap to give to the rag man.

At one point my Mum had many jobs. She made chimney pots, (more of that later), she cleaned in 3 or 4 houses and she also did "the rags" which gave us some extras, because any visitor, friend or relation would sit down with you and help with the rags.

They would deliver the boxes full of rags to our flat and Mum, with others, would have to take off buttons, zips, clasps, hooks and anything else that was not just material and they then cut up the rags and put them back in the boxes.

At one point when I was working, (so post Christmas 1962) I got a job in the rag factory and my job was to get the rags out of the large bags and wash them in an industrial washing machine and then put them in the drier. When they were dry, I would then put them in boxes ready to be delivered to people such as my Mum.

On the first day, I started to working at the rag factory some of the workers kept referring to the man who looked after the machines as Bert and I got the shock of my life when I found out it was my brother Albert.

Now a lot of these clothes came from "posh" areas and some were very good. Most of my decent clothes came out of the rags, including shirts, jumpers and trousers which were better quality than we could afford to buy.

But of course, with good things there are often bad things and although we got some decent quality clothes out of the rags, it did mean that my Mum was working with a very large pair of scissors, not a great idea for somebody as volatile as my mother but it did mean that we got pretty quick on our feet and which probably helped with my football training.

In our flat we had a door going from the living room into a small lobby and then the front door, so if we were misbehaving and Mum got fed up, she would throw the scissors at us, the boys mainly. Fortunately the door would save us from a fete worse than death.

When my sister-in-law Marlene first spent some time with us, she could not believe it when Mum threw the scissors. She was also gobsmacked when Mum, who was using the poker to get the fire going, turned on us and threw the poker at either me or my brother when we gave her some lip. This was a pretty regular event then and was not seen as a big deal by any of us but when we left the flat, when I was about 16, the four panels of the door were not in very good nick and I would have thought that the council would have had to change the door.

Yet another of Mum's jobs was to clean a local church hall after any sort of party or celebration such as a wedding, a funeral or a christening and sometimes both my sister and I would go along to help. There may have been other reasons for us to go as my sister and Mother would do a quick run round the hall looking for any cash and many times they found some, and of course, there were also other perks that people left behind like beer or cakes.

Another thing that I remember about that church hall was the electric meter. Our one at home took 6d pieces but the one in the church hall was very old and only took 1d but of course you had to keep putting money in the meter or the bloody lights would go off. But there was also another perk as my sister could attend the ballet and tap dancing classes without paying; the thought of seeing my sister in a tutu could have damaged me for life!!!

Although life was hard and we managed, but at times only just. If we did not have any money to put into the meters then we did not have any gas or electric, Well sort of, as Mum had some foreign coins that fitted in the meters and although this was totally illegal, it seemed to be an accepted way of getting through the week.

When they came to empty the meters, it livened up the whole street and we would get regular updates that the gas man or the electric man was in our street and should be with us soon. They would empty the meter and take the reading and they would then count the money in front of you.

They would then take out the foreign coins and what was left made up the rebate. Now this rebate was very important as they would often come about mid week and, bearing in mind that payday was Friday, it was very welcome to get your gas or electric rebate before pay day. Now I believe that the collectors should have confiscated the foreign coins but they never did and always gave them back to you and they were kept in a tin until they were required next time. But there were times when we either had no foreign coins left or there were power cuts, which happened in the 50's quite often and the only entertainment we would have would be playing cards by candle light. On one occasion, we were all very quietly playing cards when my Mum heard a key in the lock of the front door.

Now do remember that in those days everyone had a front door key on a bit of string inside the letterbox, rather than everyone having an individual key that could get lost, so after a quick check to make sure that we were all in the flat, she went into the kitchen and got the carving knife (yes, there is a pattern of violence emerging) and stood by the door to the lobby. Now most people who thought that this could be a burglar would have shouted out or created some noise to scare off the intruder; not my Mother, she made us all be quiet and we waited with bated breath to see what would happen.

Now there must be easier ways of making a living than breaking into the house of a knife wielding woman, who wanted your testicles as a prize and possible inclusion into next week's stew and dumplings!!!

When the intruder opened the door, and was faced with a woman who stood no taller than 5 foot and a fag paper, with a very large carving knife in her hand and a rather scary look in her eyes, he had one thought, to run. The woman would not then chase him down the street holding a carving knife, would she? Wrong, yes, she would and no amount of shouting or calling to her would stop her.

So, when they realised that she was not coming back into the flat, off went my brothers in pursuit of the mad woman. Try to get a mental picture of this; imagine, first a very frightened looking man running for his life, well at least his balls, followed by the carving knife waving woman, followed by Albert, followed by Bud and possibly followed by Tel. This must have looked like a Benny Hill TV programme (which was many years later). Albert caught up with Mum near Grove Park station and got her to stop, to the enormous relief of the intruder, I imagine.

The whole incident broke the boredom of the power cut to the enormous amusement of the neighbours and the whole bloody street, but I do not believe that this bloke was a local man, remember don't shit on your own doorstep. I think he must have just been passing when he saw no lights on and thought what a great opportunity this was, wrong again!!!

Chapter Four - School, The Cane & Bombs

On another occasion, there was a severe thunderstorm which caused a power cut (not unusual) so again we started to play cards. There was an almighty flash of lightening followed by a huge crash of thunder, followed very closely by our neighbour from upstairs, Mrs W. (she was a nice Irish lady who was a devout Catholic) came rushing into our living room and dived under the table citing 'Jesus, Mary and Joseph, save us' and my Dad, replying in a very casual manor said "You won't find him under there Tessa", which brought howls of laughter from everyone! But do remember that in those days most of your neighbours were also your best friends. They would help you in all kinds of situations from births to death and even help you to make food for a wedding reception buffet.

I loved my primary and second junior school. Mum took me out of my first junior school after the teacher smacked me around the ear with his hand. When Mum saw the mark on my face, she immediately went to the school to confront the poor terrified teacher and threatened to do the same to him. She then ensured that I changed schools and, although the new school was a bit further away, it was a lot better than the other school.

I remember that every morning we had a school assembly and we would have to pray and sing two or three hymns. Now I have never had the best of a singing voices but I loved singing and put a lot of effort into any song or hymn I sang. On one occasion the headmaster stopped the singing half way through a hymn to loudly exclaim "Who is that?" and went on to say that somebody was out of tune and hanging on the notes for far too long. He added that this person should be removed from the assembly immediately so that the rest of the school could get on and sing it properly. Yep, you know who that child was and to be honest I do not remember the incident upsetting me in any way, and I had forgotten all about that incident till recently.

My voice must have improved with age as I heard a lady comment after hearing me sing that she had never heard anything like it in her life! So, it must have been good!!! My sister says that I have such a good voice that I should keep my mouth closed to save it!!!

Apart from that incident, which was not as traumatic as it sounds, I did love my junior school. Most of the staff were very nice and as it was a small school, all the pupils seemed to know each other and we all got on very well, as far as I can remember.

The new senior school was called Mallory, which was called the "Glass School" as it had not been built long and had ceiling to floor glass windows. When seen from the road it gave the impression that it was built of glass. It had quite large grounds and was close to both Downham Way and Grove Park Station. It also had different "Houses" which I had never heard of before and if I remember correctly, I was in Galahad House. Why the bloody hell they were called houses I shell never know.

When I started at the senior school I was bought a pair of long trousers, because up until that time I only had shorts. This was not because we were poor; it was because most junior schools had shorts as part of their uniform. Of course, mine were very cheap as they were "hand me downs" from my elder brother, as were most of my clothes, but as we were used to them. Some boys carried on wearing shorts even when they started at their senior school.

It was only when I started at the new senior school that I seemed to lose my way and I got left behind both academically and socially. The only way to keep face within my peer group was to be disruptive in most lessons with one or two exceptions, such as History, Geography and Woodwork, which I was totally bloody useless at and have been ever since but I did like the teacher and that was because those subjects had good teachers. Unlike the other teachers, the Maths and English teachers - I will not name them but I do remember their names - who were totally useless and should not have been teaching children. If you were not sure about anything and made the mistake of asking, then you were ridiculed by the teacher who thought, and often said, that "if you cannot grasp that piece of information then you must be thick". I always believed that to be true (some will say it is true!) and I continued to believe it until I joined the army.

I was always doing something silly and at school I was always in trouble. For example, I had only been at the school a couple of weeks when the English teacher thought that it would be great fun to keep me behind in detention for some minor misdemeanour. My brother Terry came looking for me and told the teacher that as it was a Friday, we had to go straight home to help Mother with the shopping. But the teacher started shouting at Terry and ended up throwing a chair at him. Terry lost his rag, picked up the chair and threw it at the teacher, then grabbed me and we both ran out of the class and out of the school. For the life of me I do not think anything happened to us regarding this incident when we went back to school on the Monday morning,

Apart from the fact that the teacher never liked me and classed me the same as my brother, which in our case was fair enough, he would take every opportunity to give me 'six' of the best.

Another example was that we had a stand-in maths teacher who had just come out of the Royal Navy and had been used to teaching sailors who would do as they were told. I would have thought that most of them wanted to be there to learn, but we did not. We mucked him about something rotten and it culminated in a few of us tying him up and then locking him in the stationary cupboard and then we went home, leaving him to be found by the cleaners. This sounds horrific now and as I am writing this I would think that in society today, all six of us would have been expelled from the school, reported to the police and most probably charged with assault. We could have had a police record for the rest of our lives, so I suppose that the following punishment that we received let us off very lightly.

The result of the above escapade was for all of us, about six if I remember correctly, to be caned on the stage at assembly in front of the whole school. This was meant to make us look foolish in front of our peers and the headmaster thought that we would then be isolated by the other kids and that would stop any further trouble.

Well, he could not have got it more wrong and, as we waited to get caned, John whispered to the rest of us "whatever you do, don't cry and smile as you leave the stage". This is what we did and all the kids started clapping when we left the stage, with the headmaster going ballistic as his plan went to pieces and we were seen to be the heroes!

A good lesson to take from this is, do not try to make children look silly as you will lose respect and they will gain respect from their peers.

Do remember that in those days corporal punishment was a way of keeping good order and discipline. There was of course the cane with which you could get six strokes and for some weird and obscure reason they called it "*6 of the best*". Who bloody thought of that? Six of the best types of what? Pain, eye watering or maybe six of the best arse tingles, that no money can buy or six of the best marks that your arse will ever get.

The blackboard rubbers in those days were made from rather heavy wood with a soft material on the bottom. If the teacher was cleaning the blackboard and heard you talking or giggling, he would turn around and throw this block of wood at your head and sometimes it even hit.

Another form of punishment was the ruler. You could get a couple of strokes across the palm of your hand or more likely if the teacher was walking around the classroom and saw you mucking about or passing notes then, smack across the back of your knuckles. The sad thing was that this was ordinary, everyday life and nobody, children or adult, thought for one moment that this was odd.

Our next Maths teacher was a lot stricter. I still remember him but I will just call him Mr H and in fact I met him about 10 years later in a pub near to where I was living. Mr H had a very large plimsoll that he called uncle George, I think that is what he called it. When I first met the teacher and I am sure giving him a bit of lip, he asked me if I would like to meet uncle George. Now being a personable type of lad I immediately said that I would love to meet him and low and behold my arse was sore for the rest of the day.

I do remember the Head of Year getting us all together to see what optional lessons we wanted to do the following year. Remember that back then there was no such thing as equality for either gender and I remember a young lady who put her hand up to do woodwork and was told in no uncertain fashion that woodwork was for boys only.

I am sure you know what is coming next and yes, you would be right to think that a friend and myself put up our hands to do Domestic Science, to be told that it was for girls only! But never being two to give up, we then put up our hand for typing. By this time the teacher was really pissed off and said ok we could do it. Well, I think we went to two or maybe three lessons, caused total disruption and were both thrown out of typing class. Oh well, that is life and just another class to be thrown out of.

The science lessons were quite good but I was often thrown out of that class too for trying to set light to my mates with the Bunsen burner. Some teachers did not share my sense of humour !! But some lessons were a lot more interesting than others and the lesson on how to make a bomb (I can hear you saying, oh my god) was very interesting and I paid absolute attention throughout.

Over the next few weeks Ginger H, a school friend of mine (I think that was his name, he lived in a semi on the corner on the way to school) and I decided to collect the required ingredients to try and make our very own bomb (I can see you cringing already).

As we collected the ingredients to make the bomb, we started to experiment by making small fireworks and this made us realise that to get the stuff to explode we had to use a metal tube as the heat was just melting plastic bottles. (I know, it worried my mother as well).

We managed to get a length of scaffold pole and cut it to about 18 inches in length. We then burred over one end and drilled a hole in the middle for the fuse (I think we did the drilling in school or at Ginger's house) and we then had to get the mixture into the tube and seal the other end. We did this in our back garden, now we were not entirely stupid. Yea, ok we may have been!! As we poured the dry mixture into the tube and realised that if we started hitting the end with a hammer a spark could cause an explosion, so we wrapped it in a bit of cloth, clever ah! Education works!!

At last we had made our bomb. If I remember rightly it was about a 4lb bomb but we did not know where it was best to set it off and in the end, we decided to do it in our back garden. Now don't forget that we lived in flats. The bottom 2 flats had a garden outside their back door, the 2 middle flats (ours) had a garden backing on to the downstairs flat's garden and the top flats had their gardens backing onto ours, in a row, going away from the building, is that clear?

Now we decided that we did not want this 4lb bomb to be heard by people (I know, I know) so we decided to dig a hole and place the bomb into the hole. Our plan was to light the fuse and then run into the building for cover. At this point I do not think that we had thought this through very well as this is what happened.

Firstly, we lit the fuse and then ran towards the building to take cover. It was at this point that my niece Lorraine, aged about 4 or 5, decided to come out on the balcony to see what Uncle Keith and his friend were doing.

We shouted at Lorraine to go inside but to no avail. The fuse was now going like the clappers towards the bomb with no chance at all of stopping it. So, being brave little soldiers (which stood me in good stead for when I did join the army) we left Lorraine on the balcony and took cover.

At this point I must say in our defence that we had no idea that by putting the bomb in a hole, we were in fact making it worse and that the explosion could cause some structural damage to the block of flats and beyond, and the fact that a 4lb bomb is quite big.

When the explosion happened, I must admit that both myself and Ginge were very shocked on what a big explosion we had created. The first thing that Ginge did was to run home like bloody mad, leaving me to take the flak. Then there was Lorraine, bless her, they got her inside but she was so shocked (yes, shell shocked) that she could not speak at all. I am not sure how long this lasted but I know that Albert and Jean wanted to kill me, but common sense prevailed.

Lorraine had left the back door open on the balcony where she was stood and when the bomb went off, a fair-sized lump of rock came flying across the balcony, through the open back door and landed in the sugar bowl, which upset the family. But the most frightening thing was that if anyone, including Lorraine, had been in the way and been hit by that lump of rock, they would have been dead!!!!

Now, while we were playing bombs, the old lady downstairs was at her sink which faced the garden, filling her kettle for a cup of tea. When my Mum went down to see if she was ok, she found her to be shocked and surprised but without any injury. She did say to mum that she was stood in her kitchen and the next thing she remembered was being blown into her living room and (luckily) landed on her settee still holding her half-filled kettle.

I know that this sounds cruel, but to this day when I think of the image of an old lady flying through the air, but keeping a firm grip on the kettle, it makes me laugh. Oh, what joy!

This bomb shook houses for a fair old distance including the streets to the side, front and rear of us and very soon there were police cars and gas board vans roaming the streets thinking that it may have been a gas explosion.

I was grounded for ages and although most of the family and the neighbours wanted me hung, drawn and quartered, I got away with it relatively lightly. And Ginge? He spent ages telling his Mum and Dad that the reason he was late home was because there had been an explosion on another part of the estate and he got away with it. They pampered him as they could see that this explosion had shocked him but little did they know that he was partially to blame!!

I think my Mum complained to the school but as far as I remember nothing happened. They did stop teaching kids how to make bombs, which I suppose we should all be thankful for in this day and age.

As I said earlier, I was not a very good pupil at senior school so for the life of me I cannot think why the Headmaster asked me to look after a new boy to the school, who was in both my house and in my year. The boy's name was Tony and he was black and had just arrived from the Caribbean with his family, I think.

Tony was the first black kid in any of our local schools and was treated with suspicion by most parents, although in my house we had so many waifs and strays, so nobody noticed or thought it unusual that there was a black child in the house.

Tony was a bit of a free spirit and unfortunately, he got into the wrong company, me. I think his parents took him away from our school, as I cannot remember him being there very long.

But of course, while he was there we managed between us to create havoc and got up to all sorts of mischief, including smoking around the back of the school where some teachers would try to catch us by looking out of a high window. But as those windows were so rarely opened that when they were, they made a load of noise.

By the time the teachers got the window opened, we had either run off or were sat around like butter wouldn't melt in our mouths.

I am sure that you can see from all the above events that the school was very happy when I did not attend and were absolutely bloody delighted when my time came to leave school. It would not surprise me to hear that the teachers had a massive party to celebrate my leaving, bless 'em!

I started to smoke at about the age of 12 and most working class Londoners smoked Players Weights. Some bright spark worked out that "Weights" meant "When England Invaded Germany, Hitler's Troops Surrendered". Please do not ask me how or why I remembered this.

Of course, at 12 I could not afford many fags (cigarettes) so one way of being able to smoke was to nick the dog ends left in the ashtray by Mum, buy some cigarette papers and roll my own using the tobacco from the dog ends. This was ok if Mum had enough money to buy her fags. If she was a bit skint then she would save her own dog ends so that she could have a roll-up if she had no other fags.

When I could afford to buy fags, I had to make sure that other members of the family did not take them, so I cut a hole in the middle pages of an old book and hid the fags in there. Back then you could buy 5 fags and even 4 fags; I think they were Dunhill Domino's. In fact, most of the local shops near to the senior schools would stock packets of 4 or 5 fags mainly for the kids to buy, as they were of course cheaper than the larger packets and easier for the kids to hide from their teachers or parents.

The school decided that they would take all the identified smokers on a day trip to London to see a film about the effects of smoking. You know the sort of thing, pictures of diseased lungs, old boys who could not walk more than a couple of yards without getting out of breath etc. It did go on a bit, so after about an hour two friends and I had to go to the toilet to have a fag!!! But at least we got to spend the whole day on a nice bus trip to the centre of London and of course, we were heartbroken at having missed school for the day!

Remember, in those days we left school at 15 but life was a bit of a struggle, so for most of the year after my 14'th birthday I only went to school on occasion, mainly to play football. But in the end, they said that if I did not attend school full time, I could not play for the school team. I was only a fringe player anyway, so if that was the choice, then stick your rotten old school football team and I went up the market more often. Of course, you had to be careful that the School Board man did not catch you.

The School Board man was a bit like a Social Worker and if you were off school the school would report you to him and he would come around to your house to see if you were either not well or you were hopping the wag. But they not only went to where you lived.

They also knew where the local kids tended to hang out and gather in the parks, the markets or even in places like the station car par as all these places had various escape routes. If somebody saw the School Board man, they would either shout it out or whisper it to be passed on depending where they were and then of course by the time he got to your location you had long since gone. But to be honest I am sure that the school did not report me absent as they enjoyed it when I was not there and they did not want the School Board man to take me back into school to create more havoc.

There was always a strong work ethic within my family. Mum had 3 or 4 cleaning jobs on the go at the same time and Albert had 2 or 3 jobs as well. We have never been afraid of work.

When I was 12 years of age and a little skinny thing (my brothers always offered to play Annie Laurie on my ribs as they stuck out a bit) I got a job carrying sacks of logs from the lorry into peoples' houses or gardens and they were very heavy.

Remember that in those days not everyone could afford coal so many people bought a bag of logs on the Saturday and they were at least warm over the week-end. We also had a few flats on our round and all the other lads hated the flats as you had to go up 2 or 3 flights of stairs to deliver the logs but I loved it!! Whenever we went near the flats the other kids would ask me if I wanted to do them and I would agree.

I was paid 7/6 (that's Seven shillings and Six pence) about 38p in current money but I could make another 5/- (25p) in tips. When I went up the flats they felt so sorry for this little skinny lad that they would not only give me a very good tip but they would also try and feed me up with cake, biscuits, pies or sandwiches so I never had to spend any of my wages on food.

Chapter Five - Play, More Violence & Christmas

During the school holidays, I would go with one or two of my mates and we would take the train to Dunton Green and go fruit picking. We went to the same farm each year for three years and every year the farmer would look out for us, as there were often loads of people trying to get a job as fruit or vegetables pickers. On the last occasion when we went to the farm there was a very long queue and we thought that we would have no chance, but as we walked to the back of the queue the farmer came along on his tractor and recognised us straight away. He told us to jump on the back of the trailer and we drove past the queue to the farmhouse.

I think the farmer's name was Mr Salmon and he was always very good to us. Very often his wife would give us a sack of miss-shaped or partially damaged fruit or vegetables on top of our pay, which also saved the family money. But one time we were on the train to go fruit picking, my eldest brother Albert, who worked on the railways, was on the same train as us. Unbeknown to me, he saw us, crept up on me and gave me a wallop round the head as he had caught me smoking. Yes, another violent painful memory!

So, at 12 years of age in the holidays I would be picking fruit from Monday to Friday and then delivering logs on a Saturday. As it got closer to Christmas we would do all day Saturday and Sundays, but as I got older I gave it up and went to the markets as I could get more money. I would often take home a bag of veg that the boss or his lovely wife had given me.

Another thing that was a bit strange was that at twelve I would go to the dentist on my own and when they told me that I had to go to Guys Hospital to have a couple of wisdom teeth removed, I also went on my own. But I do feel that they took advantage of a twelve-year old as the dentist suggested that the trainees could do the extraction. Oh, yea and who thought of that!

The first bloke pulled and pulled and I could have told him that would not work but he thought he would try again and even though a couple of the other trainees were trying to hold me in the chair, he still managed to pull me right out of the chair. It was at this point that the dentist decided enough was enough and showed him how to do it. With a little twist of his wrist the bloody tooth came out and to be fair, the dentist then decided to pull out the other one as well saving me an enormous amount of pain.

Back to the food, do you notice a pattern emerging that, as a rather skinny young lad the wives of farmers, market stall holders or any female adult always felt sorry for me and wanted to feed me up, hence loads of free food from those sources!

As always, most of this book seems to be around either food or violence which I suppose sums up most of my childhood. And, of course that was why the teeth got buggered up.

My sister Bubs was given a very large white rabbit called Fluffy, (you know where this is going already) which was kept in it's hutch in the garden. When we came home from school one day Mum took Bubs aside and explained that Fluffy had got out of his hutch and has gone to join all the other bunnies in the fields, which is a lot nicer for Fluffy, and although upset, Bubs seemed to accept this explanation.

When my sister-in-law Jean returned from work that evening she could smell the cooking as she entered the flats. This was unusual on a mid-week evening as most people could not afford big meals. When she got in our flat Mum very quickly told her about Fluffy and that as Bubs was a bit upset, we would have a nice "chicken" stew for tea.

I believe it was many years before Bubs realised Fluffy's fate but in those days it was needs must. A few years later she had a dog that also disappeared, although I am pretty sure that we did not eat it!!! I just thank God that we could not afford to keep horses, who knows what would have happened there.

I was asked by Mum to go to the local shops and she gave me a pound note to get a pound of greens. Yes, I know it's easy for you to see but I spent over half an hour struggling home with a bloody huge sack of greens. But to be fair the greengrocer did ask me if I was sure that my Mum wanted £1's worth of greens or 1lb of greens and me being me, I opted for the former. What is worse is that I was made to carry the whole bloody lot back to the greengrocers and he thought it was hilarious, yeah very funny.

We always seemed to be out playing in those days and we would go home when we were hungry or when the street lights came on. Sometimes we would be out all day and take some sandwiches and a bottle of water for a picnic and head to Elmstead Woods, about a 30-minute walk away. We would make a base camp and become cowboys or Indians or commandos or whatever, but it was fun and did nobody any harm.

We did not go around stealing (ok, so maybe scrumping), painting graffiti or causing any form of criminal damage, we did not break into houses or hurt people or animals.

I would have been about eight or nine, so Terry was eleven or twelve and Bubs, yes you always had to take your little sister with you, was about five or six. Now think about this for a moment, would you let your three children aged five, eight and eleven go to the woods on their own for the whole day without any contact or means of contact, with a bottle of water and a couple of sugar sandwiches? (Do you remember them?) I doubt it and if you did, you would get reported to Social Services for neglecting your children. But we would fight off monsters in the woods, plus a few aliens and maybe even a dinosaur or two. When we did arrive home, we were filthy dirty, hungry but happy at having saved the world from a tragic end. What a sad world we now live in.

Where young children only play in an environment acceptable to adults; in the lounge or in their bedrooms, on their own with no means of socialising and not mixing with others of the same age. In the rare instance when they do go out with their mates, then their parents are also often present and they all sit around either texting each other or playing some benign game on their mobile phones and that also includes the bloody parents. How many adults have saved the world from dinosaurs I ask?

If we were not in the woods we could be down the quaggie, which is a small stream, where yet again our imaginations could run riot and we would go home very wet but happy. My Mother's view was if you came home dirty, it would wash off and if you came home soaking wet, it would soon dry.

Another of our pastimes was playing football or cricket outside the flats with the two drain holes as goalposts or the lamppost as the wicket. I was often in goal and would be the Downham Estate version of Harry Greg, the Manchester United goal keeper. Remember that there were very few cars on the roads, unlike today, and if one came along the road it would not be going very fast. One of the kids would shout out "Car" and we would grab the ball and go onto the pavement until it had passed and then get on with the game.

Oh, the freedom that we had and enjoyed will never be known by today's children and I find that rather sad.

In February 1958 I was a little over ten years of age and I loved listening to the sports report on the radio. Like many other little boys, I supported the winning high profile team of the time and that was Manchester United and I still support them to this day.

I was helping a friend's brother to deliver papers when my brother Tel came and told me that there had been a plane crash and many of the team were dead. I was devastated to find out that my hero, Duncan Edwards had died in the crash. I remember that it was in all the newspapers for weeks after the crash because many people were following the fate of Matt Busby, who was seriously hurt but made a slow and full recovery.

Over the next couple of years I went to a few live football games, the nearest professional club to us was Millwall and I vividly remember going to see them play in the FA cup. I am not sure who I went with but I think it may have been one of my elder brothers. When the visitors scored a rather brilliant goal, a Millwall supporter clapped and shouted "great goal" and another Millwall supporter was so miffed at this that he smashed a beer bottle over the man's head. It was at this point that we left, never to return, but as a Manchester United fan it did not bother me.

I still liked going to football matches so we decided to go to Charlton instead. The crowds were a lot more sedate and the atmosphere was friendly. Their ground was massive, with row after row of terracing that seemed to a young lad to reach the sky.

Other things we did included going to the beach. Yes, in London and by the Thames, at Greenwich, not far from the Cutty Sark, which was a rather large Tea Clipper that used to trade across the world. When it came to the end of its natural life, it was put in dry dock at Greenwich and has become a very famous tourist attraction and in fact the London Marathon course goes around the ship.

There was a fairly large beach and all the kids used to go there to swim. Now I must point out that the water in the Thames at that time was not very clean and very often you would notice or hear someone shout out that there was a "Richard" (a 'Richard the Third' was a turd or faeces, as we would now say) and we would wait for it to float by.

Also, very close to the Cutty Sark was a tunnel, which goes under the Thames to the Isle of Dogs and we used to have great fun going down there because it echoed and we would make ghost noises and try to scare the girls. It was also a great place to go if it was raining or very foggy, as we could play down there for hours or at least until the rain had stopped or a type of Warden would appear and throw us out.

Yet another pastime was going on the train. Now do remember that the trains back then were made up of several individual carriages, with no means of getting from one to another, unless the train stopped at a station and you could then jump out and go to another one where your mates might be. On one occasion, we were travelling home and our train stopped at the signals, as did a train going the other way. My friend Joey suggested that all four of us drop our trousers and pants and show, what looked like a carriage full of women, what little boys' willies looked like. Some just smiled and I suspect that they had sons and some covered their faces or turned their heads or just went very red in the face. But they could not tell anyone about it until they got to the next station and of course by that time, we would have left the train at Grove Park Station.

We would walk from home to the golf course, which I think was at Sundridge Park and we would sneak into the rough wooded area where we would look for golf balls. The club was aware that we did this and would encourage us to sell them to their shop for a few pennies. Of course, the man in the shop would sell them to members for a lot more than he gave us. So, we were all happy, but what he did not know was that we would hide near the fairway and if a ball came near us, we would quickly get the ball and hide again before the golfer came into sight. It was funny to watch this bloke going backwards and forwards looking for his balls (sorry ball), but of course we were not the only ones doing it, so we had to say which hole or holes we were going to cover and other kids would do the same.

There was also the "Red Rover" which was a very inexpensive bus pass and allowed you unlimited day travel all over London. I believe that myself and Joey P did in fact once get to Epping Forest and my sister and our nephew used them to go all over London. Remember this was very exciting for a child and they would stay out all day and the adults also enjoyed a day of peace.

My older brothers would also spend the day going on the Woolwich Ferry. For those of you who do not know London, the Woolwich Ferry was, and I believe still, is a free ferry and was a way of getting over to East London without having to go into town, to cross a bridge or use the Blackwall or Rotherhithe tunnels. The ferry was free so they would end up going backwards and forwards on the ferry for a large part of the day, so that they thought that they were on a bloody world cruise.

Another day out that the kids looked forward to was the fun fair on Blackheath. Wow this was very exciting for young children and we would go to look at all the different rides, plus all the stalls with their fantastic prizes. Well, we thought that they were fantastic at the time! Of course, we did not have the money to go on many rides; maybe just one or two. The bumper cars were my favourite but sometimes, if we just looked at a ride, and if it was not busy at the time, the operator would let us have a free go!!

If you continued over Blackheath into Greenwich Park it was not a lot further to walk to get to the Maritime Museum, which again was free to enter and as a young lad I found it all so very exciting. Sometimes, if the weather was not very good or if there were too many "Richards" at the beach, we would go to the Maritime Museum before going home.

Another free place to go if you liked animals was a place in Catford on a corner by Brownhill Road, known to us kids as Pets' Corner. They had all sorts of animals for sale from puppies and kittens, to rabbits and hamsters and although we could not afford to buy any, they gave us a great deal of pleasure and entertainment just looking at them and feeling very envious of those who could afford to buy a puppy or a kitten.

There were loads of parks not that far from where we lived. Some were within walking distance and some we had to get a bus.

The closest were Chinbrook Meadows, where we went to the quaggie, and there was also a very large paddling pool there where we often went in the summer when we were younger.

The rather large park next to Downham Way swimming baths, was called Durham Hill which did not have a lot there, but was good in the snow for using a tea tray to slide down the rather steep hill. Another very large park was Beckingham Place Park and of course, if we had any money, we could go to Peter Pan's Pool where we would go on the boating pond.

Although we did not have phones, computers, ipads or play stations we still had enough to do and to fill our time when we were not in school. Saturday morning pictures at what we called the Bug Hutch, but the correct name was "The Splendid" which does sound rather posh but believe me it was not. We paid 6d about 3p in today's money and we watched films for at least 2 hours and sometimes longer.

There was another picture house in Bromley and most of the time that would cost 10d and on one occasion we got very excited because the new super duper film called "Ben Hur" was being shown. But when we got there we were told that the price had gone up to 1/- (one shilling) for this film as it was a blockbuster. We were devastated and I burst into tears (only because my bloody brother Tel had pinched me so I cried) and the poor old manager felt awful, so let us go in and sit at the back to watch the film for 10p each! Wow, result!!!

We also had many sayings and things which make no sense now but to be honest, I am not sure how much sense they made then. For instance, we did not have a watch so if another child asked you for the time you would reply "half past kiss my arse and tuppence on the bottle".

Another of our very strange things was if you saw a hearse with a coffin in it, you would hold your collar until you saw a dog and then you could let go of your collar!!! I have since heard many variations of this from various parts of London and the rest of the country such as, hold you collar until you see a dog, cat, any 4-legged animal, blue car, red car etc., etc.

If you had finished a job properly or mixed paint correctly, then when you had finished you would say "Bobs ya Uncle" which would mean that the job was finished satisfactorily but of course that was only half the saying. The full saying would be "Bobs ya Uncle, Fanny's your Aunt"! Maybe some person reading this book will research it to find out where it comes from, as I have friends from Wales where they also said it and none of us are aware of its origins. Apparently, this was used all over the country but you can of course Google it to find out more. But as children we never travelled far, so as far as we were concerned, it was a London saying. How wrong can you be?

There's more, if you said "in this day and age" in the hope that you may win the lottery, then your reply could be "If pigs could fly". Well, as a lad we had not heard of that so we would say "If my Aunt had balls, she would be my Uncle" which would mean the same but was a little bit more basic!! Which for those of you that may know me, basic could be my middle name.

If we spoke to Mum about buying anything that she could not afford she would say, you can have that "when my boat comes in" which meant when her luck changed or if she got some form of unexpected payment from somewhere. In later years, I assumed that it came from the old fishwives whose husbands were away fishing and when their boat came in, e.g. meant when their husbands got paid when they got back to shore, they could then have their special treats.

More of my Mother's sayings were around hoping that something good would happen. For instance, if you were ill and hoped to be better in time to go to the football or if you were waiting for the result of a job interview and you told mum she would say "Pray to the Lord and keep your bowels open" and hoped it would happen. Also, if you were not well and did not feel like eating, she would try to encourage you by saying "if you don't eat then you don't shit and if you don't shit you die". Mother was very articulate and always full of encouragement and medical expertise.

Time now for a bit of violence! Although we were lucky enough to have a bath which was in its own small room, which at one point had been part of the kitchen, we only had one sink. It was in the kitchen and used for everything from peeling spuds or Murphy's as they were often called (or potatoes if you were posh), to bathing babies. As we only had a bath once a week, we were supposed to have strip washes every day. This put a strain on the daily routines. After the kids had finished our tea, we would have to strip wash prior to going to bed. It was only in later years that I thought about the fact that I am sure all the kids used the same flannel which must have been horrendous, but I will not go into details! The adults then ate and washed etc. You can see how easily this could lead to conflict in our household.

On one occasion Mum wanted to finish cooking the adults' tea and Bud wanted to make himself look beautiful (not an easy task) to go out. Mum started moaning at him and he started giving her some lip, so she warned him that "You are not too big for a clout". The silly boy replied, "Yes Mother I am to big for a clout" at which point she went to the cupboard, retrieved the large broom and promptly smacked him around the back of the head. Point proved I believe and I tell you what, he still remembers it to this day.

One of the waif and strays that Mum took in over the years was John. He lived with us and worked in the local bike shop. As far as I can remember, John was a big lad who later joined the Royal Marines, which I am sure suited him down to the ground. He came home on leave just before a bonfire night on the 5th November and decided, as a treat for all the kids, to buy a large box of fireworks. We would have our very own fireworks display too. We all gathered in the garden and John placed the large box of fireworks under the very big oak tree. John was warned to set off the fireworks away from the oak tree and to ensure that he closed the lid on the box.

John lit the first rocket, up it went, hit the top of the oak tree and came crashing straight back down, and yes you are right, it went into the main large box of fireworks as the lid had not been closed. This was always going to end in tears! There was bloody chaos; kids and adults were screaming and running in all directions, while at the same time, there was this magnificent fireworks display going on which most of the kids found to be fantastic fun.

I think to start with John was devastated but once he realised how much fun we and all the neighbours had, he felt better.

As you can imagine Christmas, from a child's point of view, was the best time of the year with expectations of lots of presents and lots of good food. But of course, from Mum's perspective it must have been a nightmare. It had to be planned months in advance and any of spare cash was converted into something for the festive season. We always had a real Christmas tree but I do not know who stole it or where it came from, but one thing was certain and that was that we did not buy it.

Most of our Christmas presents were either very small or bought months in advance. Anything bigger was purchased with the help of the provident cheque; wow, who remembers them? The 'provi' cheque as they were known, helped families who had very little money get through Christmas and other celebrations. The provi cheque had a face value (the amount that you borrowed) and in those days, most of the big shops took them. You would go to the store, collect the items you wanted and when you went to the till, you handed over the provi cheque and the amount you had spent would be subtracted and the cheque returned to you for further purchases, if you still had credit on the cheque.

You spent the next few months paying the provi man, who came to your house each week and when it was paid off you, could then get another if you needed to.

Mum had a cousin who lived very close to us but who we saw very rarely as she did not agree with my Father's religious views. Even after Dad died we hardly saw her and one Christmas I went with Mum to her house to take some presents for her children. Much to Mum's annoyance, she did not ask us in the house and kept us at the front door. She also refused to take the presents and that was the first time that we were told that husband and she had become Jehovah's Witnesses, who do not celebrate Christmas, nor gave or received presents. This upset Mum so much that as far as I know, they never spoke to each other again.

Most of our larger presents had to have a practical use so for instance, I may have got a new pair of shoes or a jacket or a jumper. All things that would have to be bought anyway so they were given as a present; very clever as we did not really rumble it at all and they just happened to be in the same colours as our school uniform, funny that!!

The other big Christmas con which I did not rumble until after I had joined the army and started talking to the other guys was the Christmas stocking. Ours always had the same sort of contents, an apple, a tangerine, some nuts, a couple of small things like a colouring book or a set of pencils and a balloon.

Now that was clever, a bloody balloon and as our stocking was a pillowcase, the balloon filled it out very well and made it look like we had more that we did.

By the time we started to open our stockings on Christmas mornings, the noise woke the whole family and everyone was up to watch the kids open their presents. But, and this was really sneaky, while we were all opening our presents, Mum or another designated adult would remove all the nuts and fruit from the stockings and put them in the appropriate fruit or nut bowl and then get the balloons out so we all thought that there were more balloons about, but in fact it was the same ones.

Christmas holds many memories, most of them either good or very funny and just one very sad one and that was the first Christmas after my Dad died. If I remember it right we did in fact spend Christmas with Aunt Win (Mum's sister) and Uncle Len in their flat in Sydenham, South London. They were very good to us in the years that followed Dad's death but the sad thing is that I cannot remember anything about any Christmas when Dad was alive. Even little snippets or any memory of fun or presents or having a Christmas Tree, it may be that I have blocked it out for various reasons.

Uncle Len was a really nice bloke, although up to his death he constantly told me and anyone else that would listen that I was always crying, always had a snotty nose and was known to all the extended family as 'Snotty-nosed Keith'. One of my lasting memories of Uncle Len is that whenever we went to his flat he was always playing the piano and he always seemed to be playing "Hang down your head Tom Dooley".

Aunt Win and Uncle Len had a bath installed in their kitchen but unlike our's, theirs was not partitioned off and, as the public baths were just around the corner, they decided that they would use it to store their coal rather than keep going downstairs to the coal cupboard.

I do remember some great parties at their house and to ensure everyone got some sleep, they had all the males (men and boys) in one bedroom and all the females (women and girls) in another bedroom. I also recall that the Aunty who lived downstairs from Len and Win was having a party but did not have a piano so the men got together and transported the piano down the stairs to the flat below. Either the next day or if it was Christmas, a couple of days later, they would haul the piano back up the stairs.

As I got older I would go with Mum on Christmas Eve to Lewisham market to buy the meat and veg for the whole Christmas period. I was always a bit baffled by the fact that we would arrive at the market and would go to the meat stall, but not to buy and not to be seen to be looking. We would sort of sneak a glance in the direction of the meat as we went by. As a teenager, I found this all very embarrassing and would try to walk a few paces behind my Mum. Now there was a good reason behind all this undercover work (I felt like a bloody spy): Mum was 1) making sure that there was meat left and 2) that there were turkey, pork and boiled bacon joints.

Do remember that in those days the shops shut on Christmas Eve, usually earlier than normal and the would not open again until the day after Boxing Day. If Christmas Eve was on a Sunday, the shops closed on

Saturday afternoon and would not open again until Wednesday morning, so you would have to stock up on everything or go without. Also, bear in mind that the market stall holders did not have fridges or freezers to keep the meat in so if they could not get rid of it by Christmas Eve they would have to take it home and either cook it so it lasted a bit longer or give it to friends or relatives.

Mum would wait until many of the stalls had started to close and the bloke on the meat stall started to look a bit worried before she would casually stroll into his stall area to ask the price of a Turkey. After laughing and starting to walk away, he would then drop the price dramatically. That was it, she had him now because not only had he gone down in price, but he also had other meat for sale and, if he did not ask a lot for that meat this very kind lady would be willing to help him out.

The result was that we would walk away from his stall freezing cold as we had been walking up and down all afternoon, but with a very warm glow as we had all our meat for the whole Christmas period for a fraction of the price you would have to pay in the shops.

Mum used to do this every year as far back as I could remember and every year the same market trader would have the same problem; poor sod I bet he hated customers like her! I am not sure if he ever realised that it was normally the same woman who would be his last customer on Christmas Eve and that she always managed to barter him down in price!! We always had the same meat - a Turkey, a leg of Pork and a rather large, nice piece of boiled bacon which we would have on Boxing day.

Chapter Six - Neighbours, Toilet paper & Odd Jobs

Christmas was always good for food, and we even had butter. Butter was available on a Sunday for tea but you were only allowed it if you just wanted bread and butter on its own. Now how many kids do you know who would have just wanted plain bread and butter? And if you did, it was spread very thinly by an adult. If you wanted jam or sugar on your bread then you had to have margarine, or axle grease, as it was known and in our house it was Echo margarine. I don't know if Echo is still going but the last time I saw it advertised it was as a cooking margarine instead of lard. Well actually I think that the lard would have tasted better but Mum did not like that new-fangled Stork so we had to have the Echo. The adverts all said that you can't tell Stork from butter, well I will not use the language that Mother used but it translated to 'oh yes total and utter crap' you can.

When I say that times were hard, I mean very hard. There were very few benefits and you had to work to get any money. It was of course the adults who bore the brunt of this but to us kids as long as we were fed and clothed what did we care? Life was fun for us but to make ends meet, many adults had to work in more than one job.

One of the things that Mum did to make money was to make chimney pots. They were made of concrete and were made in sections, about 3 or 4 sections if I remember correctly.

My first memory of the chimney pots was in the yard of Haseltine House, a small block of flats in Sydenham where Aunt Win and Uncle Len lived. Most of the flats seemed to be occupied by my Mum's sisters and she had a brother, Harry who lived not far away.

I remember as a young child going outside to watch Mum and Aunt Win mixing concrete by hand as they did not have any electric mixers, and filling the moulds that made each section of the chimney pot. They would wait for them to dry and then take them out of the mould and stack them ready for collection. These women had survived the war and they were certainly capable of surviving the hard times that came with peace.

Years later I remember Mum still doing the chimney pots at a builder's yard in Eltham, opposite the large church in the high street, and then a bit later over in a big, posh house near Eltham. I think she was certainly involved for many years and for some of that time she was also helped by my sister-in-law Jean, who still cringes to this very day about how hard it was and how it could give you blisters on your hands.

Although we lived on the Downham Estate we spent a lot of time in Sydenham mainly with Aunt Win and Uncle Len, but sometimes we would go and see my Nan. She must have died when I was quite young as I can only remember going to her house (she lived up the road opposite the children's hospital in Sydenham) on a couple of occasions, but I clearly remember the front door, which was in fact at the side of the house.

She was blind but you could not get one over her as she seemed to sense everything. My elder brother told me that, for instance, she would offer you a sweet from a tin and say "only take one". But even though she was blind, she knew if we took more and would tell us to put the others back! My eldest brother used to go around to their house when he had holes in his shoes and Granddad would take the shoes to his shed and put a new sole on them for him.

Another rather quaint custom was that children never went to funerals, even if it was a close member of the family like Nan, Granddad, Mum or Dad. Death was never discussed and even as an adult, it was not discussed in any depth. They did not believe in grieving; that only took your thoughts away from the here and now. This was shown by the fact that when someone died, you would close the front room curtains but as soon as they were buried and the funeral was over, the curtains were opened and you were all then expected to get on with life.

My Dad died on a Sunday evening and it was in fact my brother Terry's birthday. What a bloody rotten birthday present for a young lad, to know and to always remember that your Dad died on your birthday and I swear that Terry thought that Dad had done it on purpose.

We were all allowed to stay up to see the end of Sunday night at the London Palladium, but not long after we were asleep we were woken by noise and the fact that

Mum brought my sister into our room. Bud did not come to bed so I assume that he was sent round to fetch the doctor.

Remember we did not have a phone and the nearest phone box was by the doctor's surgery and the doctor came immediately. Today they would say he is dead anyway so I will pop in tomorrow.

The next morning we were told that Dad had died. We had about an hour of grieving and then it was time for school and I remember crying in class. The teacher got annoyed and asked me why I was crying and I still remember replying "you would be crying if your Dad died last night". It worked a treat, as she almost started crying as well and I was sent home, aged 10 on my own. Would that happen now? I doubt it but my Mother was not happy, as she had loads to do and did not want us in the way. I assume that his body was removed on the Monday as he was taken for a post-mortem because he had died suddenly.

So I was sent round to Mrs P in the next block of flats who was a friend of Mum's and stayed there for the rest of the day. But the next day it was back to school and as far as family were concerned, you cried yesterday so that is the grieving process over and done with.

It was the same on the day of the funeral. We were not allowed to go and I don't know to this day if anyone, apart from Mum went as it was a pauper's funeral. No cars or lots of flowers, and about three or four people in plywood coffins in one grave. I do remember my Mum saying that there was a child buried in the same grave as Dad and that he would have liked that.

It would have been better for all concerned if they had cremated the paupers instead of burying them as they would not have taken up space in the graveyard and their families could have at least had the ashes of their loved ones. We had nothing, not even a headstone, a cross or some other indication of where our father was buried, and it was from this time onward that we all had to grow up a lot quicker. I have been back to that cemetery on a few occasions and all the paupers' graves were down by the railway line but when looking some years later, I found that the paupers' graves were gone and there were many new graves with very posh headstones. Oh well, that was the way of the world at that time.

Nobody can remember going to a funeral but a pauper's funeral it was not carried out in the traditional way. I have since found out that Dad was buried on the following Saturday, which was very quick bearing in mind that he'd also had a post-mortem and as several people were being buried in the same grave, I assumed that it was done on a Saturday to avoid upsetting the paying customers. I think my Mother went but as far as we know nobody else did, although it is possible that Uncle Len or Aunt Win went for morale support.

After my Father's death, we very rarely spoke about him and he was not referred to very often by my mother, only to curse at him for dying. Most of my memories of my Father are of when he was pissed.

We sometimes went to see Uncle Harry and his daughter Maureen, who was disabled with what may have been polio. Political correctness or even sensitivity had not been thought of in those days so she was known by all the family as 'crippled Maureen' I know it is awful but they were the times we lived in but I do remember that her husband was a big man and us children thought that he was a giant! I remember the adults calling him the 'gentle giant'.

Uncle Harry was a member of the Oddfellows as was my Dad (which is sort of ok because they were both a bit odd) and when Dad died Uncle Harry was a great support to us, as was Aunt Win and Uncle Len.

He used to take us to his club which I think was in upper Sydenham but to be honest, I cannot be sure. I do know that my brother Terry won a talent competition at the club on his mouth organ and I also remember the Christmas Parties which were very good and with great presents, in fact better presents than the family could afford to give us.

Uncle Harry also arranged for Terry, Bubs and I to have a holiday for underprivileged kids at St Margaret's Bay near Dymchurch in Kent. That's funny because we did not feel underprivileged in any way but it was on this holiday that Terry reliably informed me that I was adopted. I think I cried for most of the week and when I told Mum she went mad and just in case you are not sure, no I am not adopted!

Terry told many people over the years that we were all adopted, including his own partner and children. When his partner was told that this was not true by another sister-in-law and she was told that we all had birth certificates with the names and occupations of our parents and not adoption certificates, she obviously did not believe her. Oh well, we believe what we want to believe and as Terry is no longer with us, I will not speak ill of the dead.

During the time around my Father's death there were lots of things going on and one of those was the youth club run by Mrs B in Ballamore Road school once or twice a week. It was really good fun and I used to look forward to it and of course it got me out of the house for a couple of hours in the evening.

I would get there early and help to get out the equipment and games such as the table tennis, cards and board games and I would help Mrs B cut cake and get the orange juice ready. As a reward, I would get a slice or two of the ginger cake. I never did work out why it was always ginger cake, maybe she got it cheap from someone, who knows.

When the club closed for the evening Mr Barker was always parked outside in his Ford Pilot car. Wow, this thing was big and beautiful and much admired by all the kids as it had big wide running boards either side and we all dreamed that one day we would have a car like that !!!

Some of us would help Mrs Barker take stuff to her car and help load it. We would then all hang on to the side of the car, standing on the running boards and Mr Barker would drive us home and as he got close to your house, you jumped off so by the time he got to the main road he had dropped off all the kids without even stopping the car. He had to stop doing it in the end as there were so many kids hanging on the side of his car it was getting very dodgy and could have ended up with a child getting hurt, so it was back to walking home, although this was not far it did mean going up a fairly steep but short hill.

It was winter time and there was lots of snow and ice on the ground and I had been out shopping with Mum. When we returned, we came down some steps at the side of the local church and rejoined the road at the top of that short but steep hill referred to above. At this point we saw an old lady pulling a wicker type shopping basket on wheels and as she looked down the hill she very sensibly decided that she would put the shopping basket in front of her rather than pulling it downhill.

As she got the basket in front of her and started to descend the hill, she slipped and went onto her backside but she kept hold of the basket. The next thing we knew was that both the old lady and the basket had now picked up a bit of speed and were nearly flying down the hill, her legs in the air showing off her bloomers. My Mother was horrified; 'Do something' she told me, and to my eternal shame I did do something; I nearly wet myself laughing! I could not move for laughing and as I type this out I have started giggling again!

As it happened, I did manage to stop laughing in time to go to the bottom of the hill to see if she was ok and guess what? Yep, she was still sat on the ground with her legs around the basket laughing her head off (just an expression of course) and telling me what had happened!

I did not have the heart to tell her that I had watched it all but I am sure that she enjoyed it as it must have brought back memories of her own childhood. She soon got to her feet unhurt and carried on her way, but I swear that I could still hear her giggling as she went up the road.

In those days, we were all expected to do things in or around the house, no matter what age you were. It could just be clearing the table after dinner or putting out the knives and forks ready for dinner or scrapping the leftovers (not bloody many in our house) into the bin. There was no re-cycling in those days. As you got older you would also run errands for both your family or for neighbours. It was always good running errands for neighbours as they would often give you a penny or two for going but of course you did not get anything from family.

The old lady downstairs would often ask either myself or my brother to get her some bits from the shops and would nearly always give us 3d for going. On one occasion, she asked Mum if Terry and I would dump her very old chaise lounge and she gave us a shilling for doing it, that was 6d each. But it was many years after before I realised that we were in fact fly tipping and we could have been fined. Now I am not sure if the old lady was very innocent or very crafty but it worked and she got rid of her rubbish. The sad thing is that today that chaise lounge would have been worth a lot of money.

In those days, there were no betting shops and off course betting was illegal (as most things that we got involved with were) but of course, it still went on. The bookies would stand on street corners ready to take the bets and they would have lookouts who would give a pre-determined signal if they saw a copper coming, such as putting on a flat cap or taking off the cap. The bookie would see this signal, pass the money and the bets to another runner and when the police arrived the bookie would be all sweetness and light and explain that he was just waiting for a friend who luckily would turn up at that point.

Because it was illegal and because there were times when the police caught the bookies, most people did not use their own names but used pseudonyms and my Dad's was Danny Dean. When he was taking a bet or if he had winnings to come, I would walk along the road towards the bookie and we were told that if he did not talk to us then we had to walk on past and go back later and when he did talk to you and you were collecting winnings all you said was "Danny Dean" and he would pull out a little bag and give it to you.

I never looked in the bag but I suspect that he never won very much at all but if he did then he kept it very quiet from my Mother. Dad also gambolled on the football pools. Each week someone would call to collect your pools coupon on the Thursday and give you a new one to fill out for the following week. Remember the jackpot was £75,000, which was a fortune in those days, and we would dream about how we would spend it; maybe a new house, a new car, a holiday to another country, yeh, dream on!!

In our road, we had some funny characters but they all mucked in and helped each other, or at least most of them did.

In a house opposite our flats lived Mr C and he worked in the docks. Now in those days it was a very good and very well paid job and Mr C had stuff that we could only dream of. He was the first in the road to have a car, a TV and a telephone and if anyone fell ill and you needed to phone the doctor, he was always happy for people to use his phone. We watched the coronation on his TV and remember, we are not talking 42-inch flat screen LCD TV, we are talking about a huge cabinet housing a 10-inch TV that was in black and white and because you only had an indoor aerial you had to keep moving it around to get the good picture. But Mr C was an expert at it and kept a pretty decent picture for the whole event.

We did not get a TV in our flat till about 1958, not long before my Father died and just like Mr C's, it was a bloody huge cabinet with a 10 or 12-inch screen in a rather faded black and white; in fact, it looked more like dark and light gray than black and white.

During the week, the TV did not start till 5pm with Children's Hour and that is what it was, 1 hour of children's TV only. On a Sunday I think it started about 2pm and then shut down at 5pm till 7pm and I remember we would not normally be allowed to stay up until the end of Sunday night at the London Palladium.

Now bear in mind that the programme was on till 8pm, so even my brother Terry who would have been 13, was not allowed to stay up till 8pm. My, how things are so very different now, but is it better? I am not sure.

In the flat above us were the W's and like Dad they were Irish and great fun to be around. Maureen was a friend of both Bud and Albert and she was a very attractive young lady with many gentlemen friends, one of whom was a Maltese man who owned a nightclub in Soho. He was very well known in that area in the late 50's and 60's. G was not liked by either Mr or Mrs W so when he came to pick Maureen up in numerous flash cars, including a pink Cadillac convertible, he would pay one of us to run upstairs and tell Maureen that he was waiting in the car. Depending on what sort of mood he was in he would give us anything from a shilling 1/- to half a crown 2/6, which in those days was a lot of dosh for very little work, just a nifty run up the stairs. 1/- = 5p and 2/6 = 12 and 1/2p.

Because Maureen's parents did not approve of G, they would try to stop her going out and one day when he was waiting in the car, Maureen got out of their toilet window (no mean feat on its own) and climbed down the drain pipe past other people's toilet windows. As you can imagine this could be a little discerning if you were minding your own business, reading the paper and having your early evening dump when Maureen smiles as she passes the window. Never a dull moment in our flats!

Next door to the W's on the top floor was Mrs McK. I do not know an awful lot about her except that all the neighbours called her Mrs McFlute and she was a little mad, as opposed to the distinctly sane attributes shown by the rest of the street so far. I do remember my Mother having a punch up with her next to the coal cupboards on the ground floor of the flats with all the local kids watching through the glass doors and getting very excited by it. But for the life of me, I cannot remember why they were fighting and just in case you were waiting to ask, yes Mum did win!

When John came home he asked Mum the name of the lady on the top floor and Mum told him it was Mrs McFlute, so when he saw her the next day he was very polite and said "Good morning Mrs McFlute". Well, she was not at all impressed and told him so in no uncertain terms. Mum and the rest of us just kept laughing!

In the flat next door to us was Mr and Mrs W and, like many others, he spent a lot of time in the garden looking after his vegetable patch. It was on one such occasion that my sister was on the balcony and Mr W was in his garden and he was wearing some very short, shorts and his willy was hanging out, I am not sure if this delighted or terrified my sister.

In the first house next to the flats were Mr and Mrs J. They were a nice couple who kept chickens and he also grew vegetables, which he sometimes gave to us and he gave me advice when I was growing vegetables.

Also, just up a bit from Mr C was a barber, but I am afraid that I cannot remember his name. He saved us money while at the same time earning a few bob on the side, although I am sure he would have declared his extra earnings to the tax man!!
He would cut the hair of most of the men and boys in the street and sometimes when you went to his house, you would be told to come back later as he was a bit busy.

On one occasion just before Dad's work's sports day, I was instructed to go and get a haircut. I then told the barber that I wanted what was in effect a "skinhead", although it was not called that in those days. The barber questioned if I had permission for such a haircut and I assured him I did, so he went ahead (no pun intended). Mother of course, went mad when I went home but the reality was that the barber could not stick the hair back on, so she had to accept it, although I do remember getting a wallop for lying to the barber.

Now when I say that our street was a bit strange, I do really mean that the whole bloody area was strange, not only the people that lived there but even the people that visited. I think that in this politically correct society which we live in, we could learn a lot from the past.

We had our very own "tramp". He did not have a permanent address and would sleep wherever he could find a warm spot in winter and a cool one in summer. The locals would often give him clothes or blankets and he would often get food or drinks from the residents. But to us kids he was known as 'Dog End Bennett' because he would go around the streets looking for dog ends (cigarette ends) that he would take apart and roll up in fag papers to give him a smoke. The very sad thing about Dog End Bennett was that neither the children or the adults thought he was odd and he was just accepted as the local tramp. Sometimes a local resident would tell him that they had seen a big dog end near the station or the bus stop and he would hurry off to that location to find it.

We also had an older lady that was known as the "Duchess of Downham" because she would dress in very outlandish clothes of various colours and in the main bought from a local jumble sale and things like a fur Stoll were very cheap. But she was just one of many people who lived on the estate who could be termed as a little weird.

There was also a man who had some form of learning difficulty and I think he would now be called Autistic or have Asperger's syndrome. His name was Terry and he supported a local football team, which I think was Bromley.

Terry was an encyclopaedia of football facts and as children we would shout out "who won the 1927 FA cup final?" and he would immediately come back with the names of the two teams, the score, who scored the goals and the time of the goals. He was fantastic and as far as I remember, he never got any wrong at any time. Terry was still living there when I joined the Army and left home.

We had a window cleaner (not for the flats) come down our road who was a known paedophile. Everyone knew that he would offer the boys money for whatever, I did not know. As I did not then, and still do not, allow strangers to fiddle with my willy.

The window cleaner was known as "whip it quick the bum bandit" and all the mums would threaten him with castration if he went near their kids. A little extreme I know, but it did seem to work and more importantly, everyone including the police knew where he lived and worked and he was under the constant watchful eye of the mums and dads. Nowadays they force someone out of their neighbourhood but that paedophile then moves away and nobody, including the police, knows where he is so he can then carry on abusing.

As you can guess by now, money was a bit tight when I was growing up (not that I have mentioned that very much) and very often we had to make do and mend, which did seem to make us resourceful and which, I must say has stood me in good stead ever since.

There was no way on earth that my Mother could afford to buy us all bikes, even second hand ones, so the only way we were ever going to get a bike was to make it up out of spare parts. The best place to look for these was the foot path towards the railway bridge at the end of our road. People dumped their old bikes or even parts of bikes such as an old saddle or a set of handlebars and the funny thing was that in 2003 when my brother was over from Australia, we went with my son, Glenn, who was 14 at the time, to look around the old estate. When we parked the car, and started walking down the path, Glenn asked why we were walking down there. I told him that this was the place where people used to dump their old bikes or bits of bike and we would go along and get what parts we needed to make up our own bike. As we turned a corner, there was a dumped bike laying by the edge, so they still do it now.

I remember getting together a large, heavy bike made from bits and pieces, which we found or were given. My friend Ginger and I decided on to go on an adventure and we would ride our bikes way down into Kent, to the bottom of Wrotham Hill, pronounced Routam Hill. Going down was ok but it was a bloody steep hill, so when it came time to go back up, we waited for an electric milk float to chug up the hill and we grabbed the back with one hand and were dragged up the hill.

Although the milkman saw what we were doing he just turned a blind eye and the bonus was that Ginger's Mum and Dad, who had a car, were waiting at a lay-by at the top of the hill with a picnic which was great. Although they thought we would be knackered after such a climb up that very steep hill.

We also used to look for old prams so that we could get the wheels and make go-karts, which were also a great source of entertainment and fun. But you may have noticed that most hand made go-karts had two large wheels at the back and two smaller ones at the front and the reason for this was that it was rare to find an old pram with four wheels. They would have been dumped because at least one of the wheels were knackered but they nearly always had two wheels we could take and then find another pram and get two more wheels which may have been smaller.

As I said before, we lived close to a small but fairly steep hill but at the bottom of the hill was a crossroads so we had to send one of the kids down to the bottom and they would wave when it was all clear. But remember there were not a lot of cars on the road back in the late 50's so the poor sod at the bottom of the hill would end up bored silly and would only perk up when he saw a car coming and he could stop us at least for a few minutes.

As you can imagine with over 12 people living in a 3 bedroom flat there had to be some organisational skills involved in getting all the kids up and ready for school as well as the adults needing to eat, wash and shave. Remember there was only one sink and that had to do for washing both plates and people, so every morning was like a military exercise with all of us knowing what to do and when, including when to wash and when to eat.

Because of the total mayhem in the flat, all of us had various jobs to do. I had three main jobs and they were 1) take the rubbish downstairs and put it in the main bin. I did not mind this job as it was easy and took no time at all, however, my other two jobs were more time consuming. As I said earlier, we had very little money and any purchase of shoes had to be planned and budgeted for well in advance and because of that we often had holes in our shoes. I would cut out a piece of cardboard, normally from a Kellogg's cornflake packet, and put it into the shoes. This did not make them watertight but did stop you getting holes in your socks and blisters on your feet. In fact, this required an amount of skill, as some of the shoe uppers were also pretty much worn out as were some of the feet that went in them.

In our house toilet paper was an "extra" and not an essential part of the shopping list (yes, I know what you are thinking) but we had to have some sort of alternative and that alternative was newspaper. Yes, daily newspapers had more than one function, you could read them and you could also wipe your bum on them.

As I said earlier we would collect newspapers for the fish shop to wrap fish and chips. They would put the fish and chips directly onto the newspaper and it was only many years later that they started to use grease proof paper to lay the fish and chips on first. But then they still wrapped them in newspaper and of course in time newspaper was known as a health hazard and they had to use plain white paper.

Although in some areas the locals were not happy so the chippy would use the greaseproof paper, then the plain white paper and then to keep everyone happy, they would then wrap the whole lot in newspaper. But this did not last long, although there may still be some chip shops in parts of London who still do that.

After selling some of the newspapers to Mr L, we would also keep some to use as toilet paper and my job was to fold the page of the paper in two and tear it in half and then tear it in two again, so one page of the Daily Mirror or Daily Sketch would make four pieces of toilet paper. I am sure it gave the adults loads of pleasure in wiping their bums on the face of a politician or known criminal.

But there was also a down side and that was that back in the 1950's the print came off the paper a lot easier than it does today, so after wiping you bum you had black smears everywhere. As children, you were not aware why your white underpants had black marks as well as skid marks!!! and today you could enter your pants in to the Turner Prize as they were very artistic!

When I had finished tearing up god knows how many newspapers and putting them in a neat pile, my Mum would use a big butcher's hook to make a hole through the lot and then pull though string to then hang them from the toilet roll holder. This gave us enough toilet paper for a few days and then I would then have to start the whole process again.

There were many telephone boxes all around the estate as most people did not have a phone. There were telephone directories in those boxes and if we stole one and told mum that we had found it on a bus or in the street that was ok, as they made great toilet paper. You tore out the pages and ripped them in half and made rather large sheets of toilet paper that were not only softer than the newspapers, but the ink did not come off on your bum.

Chapter Seven - Illness & Death

I would often run errands as I have already said and there was always an opportunity to either get into trouble or to try saving some money and the shops were the place for both.

I used to be sent to the shops for a large bloomer, which was a very large uncut loaf of bread. Very often it was still warm and was always crispy, so as a young lad I would break off bits of the bread and eat them on the way home. I would always get into trouble, but I never learnt as the smell of freshly baked bread was just too much of a temptation, and it still is to this day.

To try and save a few bob we would buy stale cakes (see previous pages) and broken biscuits. It was great to be asked to go and buy them as the amount of biscuits you got depended on who served you and how much they had to get rid of which is why we always left it late in the day to get as much as possible. I would try to eat all the best ones on the way home and tell Mum that this was all they had, but as I was not the only one to go and get the cakes, all the family used the same tricks. Mum always knew that, if you turned down a cake when you got home, you had already had your share.

My eldest brother Albert was the tower of strength in our house and even more so after Dad died. He was like a second Dad to us and ensured that we kept on the straight and narrow.

Albert has always had an interest in shooting (weird, I know) but that interest often kept us in meat as he would go rabbit shooting with his mates and we would reap the rewards.

Albert had a mate Les, who lived nearby and his Mum worked with my sister-in-law, Jean at the Jam factory. Both Albert and Les had a fascination with guns and Les's Dad had a Tommy Gun which he probably got during WW2. The boys tried to find ammunition to fit the gun, and luckily for us, they could not find bullets that fitted.

Albert did not drive at the time but he did have a bike and boy, was it a bike! It was a Claude Butler hand-built bike and it was superb to ride. As far as I know they still produce those fantastic cycles. Although I did not get to ride it often and in fact the only time Albert would let me ride it was if one of the younger kids was ill and the doctor had prescribed medicine outside of the normal shop hours. We would have to go to the 'out of hours' chemist, which was at the bottom of Downham Way, over a mile away. So, Albert would let me use his bike to collect the medicine. Of course, I would take my time and hope that one of my mates would see me as I posed on this very posh and expensive bike but if any harm had come to that bike I was under no illusion that Albert would kill me.

As you have already read, we had a load of relatives but in those days any friends of your parents were always known as Aunty or Uncle out of respect for the adult.

Mrs P was known to us kids as Aunty Flo and she lived a few streets away and I would go around there with Mum sometimes or take something round for Aunt Flo.

She smoked like a chimney and always had a fag dangling in her mouth. So much so that there was a huge brown stain starting on top of her lips and ended up at the side of her nose although, as a child I would swear that the stain went to the top of her head. The only time she took the fag out of her mouth was to get rid of the ash at the end and as far as I recall she always caught the ash in time and it never fell on the floor or on her mat. She would remove the fag to kiss us children but this was not the greatest of experiences, nor was it the greatest of smells, but as it was sometimes accompanied with a few pennies it was worth it!

We also had Uncle Fred living with us for a while on and off. He would go away for a short while and then come back for a few months. He too saw the rough side of my Mother's aggressive and knife wielding nature and I believe that he was chased out of the house by Mother and the carving knife. Oh, what fun us kids had watching my Mother chase the other adults with rather large knives!!!

I believe that Uncle Fred was an old friend of my Father but he was a bit scruffy and never seemed to have any money but as he was often pissed, he must have had money for booze. There was another uncle who I think was another Irish friend of my Father. His name was Uncle Joe and he was a gentle man who spoke with a soft Irish accent. My sister has a photo of Uncle Joe and her on a day out. I cannot remember having a lot to do with him but then again, I was a bit older and would prefer to be out with my mates.

My four best mates were Dave C, Geoff D, (his Dad died not long after my Dad), Les T, who lived on Downham Way and Ginger H.

Geoff, Les and Ginger went to the same senior school. But Dave went to a better school a bus ride away. They were a lot posher than us as they had a telephone, a Robin Reliant car and carpet in the living room and on their stairs, which was handy as on one occasion when we had a party at their house and I fell down the bloody stairs, pissed aged about fourteen !!!

My eldest brother Albert and his wife Jean lived with us for some time with their children. One day I was day dreaming (not unusual, and nothing has changed there even after all these years) and looking at this beautiful car, which I thought I would like to own one day. "It's no good you looking at that car because unless you buckle down at school you will never be able to afford one" said my sister-in-law Jean. Well I did not buckle down at school but I did get my Jaguar, although it was about 40 years later. I then went on to own Jaguars for the next 10 years and in fact, I have just gone back to a Jaguar which I adore.

In the late 50's and the early 60's we all got up to various forms of mischief and we were no different from the rest, but my brother Terry seemed to be doing more than the rest of us or he was getting caught more than us, I am not sure which. But Terry was always in some form of trouble and often with the police. One day two policemen came to the flat and wanted to talk to Terry. One of the coppers had been to our house a few times before and Mum found him to be very rude and a bit arrogant.

Mum allowed the nice copper in but said "no" to the other one. The copper said "You can't stop me coming in". "Oh, yes I can" said Mother and slammed the door on the copper's foot, which, not surprisingly, he then removed. I am sure that his mate smiled but did not comment either way.

This part of the story will carry on in a moment, but to set the scene, we must remember that in those days most women knitted for their families and because they could not always afford to buy wool, they would get old jumpers or cardigans and re-knit the wool. For instance, the jumper may have had a stain or a hole so they would unwind the wool and use all that they could. The kids were made to sit with their arms outstretched and Mum would start to unpick the wool from a jumper and wind the wool around our arms to stop it getting tangled. Most of us hated that as it made your arms ache and Mum would moan at us (or was it just me) for being weaklings. They would knit hats, scarves, swimming trunks (yes, I know that wool does not react well to getting wet and you end up with the crutch around your ankles), jumpers and tank tops. As they only had a limited amount of wool, the jumpers or tank tops would be of multiple colours and someone like my Mother could knit at great speed, not even looking as they knitted. She could hold a conversation or listen to the radio or even watch TV all while knitting and in fact, she carried on knitting right up until her death in 1971. In the main she was knitting things for grandchildren, with the occasional scarf for a friend or neighbour.

I must admit that there are times when the constant *click click* of knitting needles does drive you to distraction. But I must say that they made great daggers when fighting with my brother and I swear that I still have potholes caused by knitting needles that were not thrown by my Mother.

We now return to Terry and his ability to get into trouble while trying to be nice to others, remember the incident with the flowers at the cemetery?

My sister-in-law, Jean would hang her nylons on the line to dry and every now and then a pair would go missing. It was only when a lady from down the road came to our flat and asked Jean if Terry had any more of those cheap nylons that he had been selling, that she knew where they had gone!!!! He could have been a great business man with that "I can sell anything" attitude, although I am not sure that Jean would agree.

It was coming up to Mum's birthday and like most children we had very little money and were forced to use our imagination or other skills to ensure that Mum got a present on the day.

Terry surprised everyone by buying Mum a knitting machine for her birthday. Wow, now I am not sure when or who discovered that the gas meter had been broken into and all the money stolen. It was more difficult to detect because the thief cut up a cereal box and placed it in the meter so when you put in a coin it did not make the meter sound empty.

Now you did not need to be a master detective to put two and two together and come up with the name of Terry, which everyone did, including the police, and Terry was subsequently arrested and charged. I am not sure of the outcome on this occasion but in those days Borstal was a short, sharp shock to the system and was designed to make it so uncomfortable that inmates would not re-offend. The length of detention in Borstal, in the main, only lasted for about 6 or 9 months and I believe that was enough. Approved Schools, which were not as tough as Borstal, used other gentler methods to try to rehabilitate young lads who had broken the law. Terry spent time in Mayfield in Sussex, where I visited him with Mum and in Doncaster, Yorkshire.

He also did some time in prison in Wormwood Scrubs (a London prison) where I visited him, but I don't think he spent long in there. I do not remember what he had done that time and I am not sure what happened to the knitting machine, but maybe it was sold to pay back the gas board.

As I mentioned earlier, we relied on the Provident cheque to get through Christmas but the rest of the year we relied on the "tally man". He would bring all sorts of goods to the door and try to get you to buy them and pay an amount each week for them and known to most people as the "never, never" as you never did seem to pay it off. As we did not always have the money to pay him, we were told to sit still and be quiet until he had gone. We were lucky because we lived in a flat and we did not have to hide as he could not walk around and look in the windows. But we were not allowed near the windows just in case the tally man saw us.

I got my first suit from the tally man for my brother Bud's wedding. It was a tiger tooth grey check and I was very chuffed to look so smart. Without the tally man, I would have never been able to afford a suit.

I was always ill as a child and, if there was anything going around, not only would I catch it but I would end up in hospital. I must have been about 7 years old when I collapsed on the way to Ballamore School. I was in a lot of pain but they did not fuss a lot in those days and nothing so caring as getting an ambulance. No, one of the other kids ran back to my house and told my Mum and, when she arrived and saw the swelling, she realised it was not a scam to get out of going to school.

I was taken to the Doctor and then sent to the hospital. By the time we got to the hospital, the swelling had gone down and they would not operate until they knew which side the hernia was on for certain.

In line with the warm and caring attitudes of the time, I was made to run around the ward and up and down stairs until the swelling re-appeared so they could see which side it was on and they could then operate. I was in agony. That was modern day technology which young people today cannot seem to get their heads around. My sons often think that we were brought up in the dark ages and to an extent I suppose we were. We would have seen mobile phones, ipads, computers and of course, laptops as pure science fiction and if you had told us that those things would be with us over the next few decades, you would have been laughed out of the room.

One of the good things about being poor and being in hospital, apart from getting a bath every day and three meals a day which did seem a little unfair to me because as I was ill I did not feel like eating, life can be very cruel sometimes. Another thing was that when you were discharged from hospital, you were sent on convalescence, to places as far away as Broadstairs, Hailsham, Herne Bay and Deal, not quite exotic but it was for me as I had never been very far off the estate where we lived and to a young lad this was just a holiday. The irony is that I now live very close to Broadstairs and Herne Bay!

The first place that I remember going to was Broadstairs in Kent, where my sister now lives. I have never found the place where I was sent but I can still see the building in my mind. It was large, rendered and white and I was very upset when my Dad left. A male nurse gave me an old watch to with which to play and I soon forgot about home. What a cheapskate I was, forgetting home for a broken old watch, wow!

I cannot remember all the different things which were wrong with me, but I do remember going to both Herne Bay and Hailsham twice.

To this day, I remember Judy, a smashing nurse who looked after me very well during both visits to Herne Bay. Her boyfriend was in the Navy and about that time there was a pop song the words which we changed slightly:

> Judy oh Judy, Judy don't let me down,
> Write me a letter soon or I'll be homeward bound

I cannot swear to it but I have an idea that his name was Freddie and he was a Navy boxing champion. I went back there about a year later and Judy was still there. She was what I now call 'a very old fashioned, kind and caring young lady' who seemed to love her work and all the kids she cared for. Bear in mind that they were not all well behaved and most of us were not all sweetness and light, but she still managed to treat us all the same and with kindness.

Another place I went to twice was Hailsham in Sussex. I can still picture the farmhouse kitchen with it's very large table which we used to all sit around and as far as I can remember, there were other kids who were also on convalescence. The food was fantastic, more than I was ever used to; no wonder I was always ill. Every place I went on convalescence the food was not only very good, but there was lots of it. The staff in those places would see a skinny little lad who needed feeding up to help him get over his illness, yep, another result!

The place in Hailsham was a working farm and the people there were very kind. As it was my birthday, they encouraged my Mum and Dad to visit but it was a fair old trek from the road, across the fields full of cows and up the hill to the farmhouse. As we knew what time bus they were coming on, we took some wellies down to the bus stop to meet them and on the way back through the field of cows, my Mother got stuck and could not move.

The cows in the field were friendly but curious and when this woman started to shout that she was stuck, they all decided to wander over and have a look. Now this got Mum a bit more uptight, which was not helped by my Dad and the children all laughing at her! In the end, it was the farmer who came over, got rid of the cows and rescued Mother.

The last place I went to was Deal in Kent. It was a large, terraced house just back from the sea and again, I can still see it in my mind and have in fact. passed it several times in recent years.

The man who was in charge of the house would give us little jobs to do and pay us for doing them. I got a 1/- for fluffing up his pillows for a week; another child got a 1/- for cleaning his shoes and for those of us who arrived without any money, it gave us a chance to get our ice cream money.

The Broadstairs and Herne Bay places were run by nurses and I assume were part of the new NHS. They may have been nurses but they did not wear any uniform. Hailsham was a working farm run by farmers and Deal was the same. The man in charge was tall and very well built, and he was liked by all the children because as far as I remember, he was a kind, jolly man with a good sense of humour.

I thought that going to the seaside or country after being ill was great. It was all arranged for you by what was then known as the hospital almoner, or in other words the hospital social worker. They would ensure that you had rail passes for both an adult and me, plus money for food or buses at either end of the journey.

To this day, I can remember the area where the almoner had her office (they were not all female but this one was) and the waiting area at St John's Hospital near Lewisham in South London, where I had my hernia operation. I was in hospital for nearly two weeks but nowadays you would be in have the operation and be back home in a few days.

In those days, your local doctor's surgery had one doctor with a quite large waiting room where the secretary/receptionist sat. You did not get any an allocated number; you were just told that you would follow Mrs Smith and when she went in to see the doctor you knew it was your turn next.

We had the same doctor for at least ten years, I will call him Doctor A. He smoked like a trooper and drove a car called a Mayflower.

When it was your turn to see him, he would put his fag in the ashtray while he examined you, but while he was talking to you or writing out a prescription, he would then continue smoking. Health and Safety at its best! But in those days, everyone thought it was normal, unless of course you had a rotten cough, then you may have been a bit pissed off.

The great thing about the doctors in those days were that they seemed to work night and day, so if you called out the doctor at night, they knew that it was an emergency.

He would always come immediately and nine times out of ten he would tell you that you had done the right thing by calling him out and he did not make you feel stupid. Wow, what a difference to today!!!

Chapter Eight - Family, Relatives & Smog

I was often off school sick and remember going with Mum to the National Assistance Office. She told me it was to claim her Widow's Allowance but in truth, she was never married to my Dad, although I did not find this out till many years later when she wanted to re-marry. She told me then that she did not have a Widow's pension but it was in fact a National Assistance Allowance. Although I went with her, I did not go into the office so that is why I never knew.

I also went with her to an office which I think was above Woolworths at the bottom of Downham Way. I think it was the British Legion who gave her some financial help.

I was a bit shocked to find out so many bits and pieces about both my Mum and Dad and the rather colourful life they had led, about which to this day we know very little. In recent years a cousin, Charlie, the son of one of Dad's brothers, contacted us and we have learnt a lot about the family from cousin Charlie and his wife Julie. They are a smashing couple and it was his father, Dermot who was given away as a child (see below).

It must have been difficult for Charlie and Julie to trace us, as I had changed my name from Cooke to Coleman-Cooke to include my wife's maiden name. But they still found us with the help of the Internet and Google, which made it much easier. Having said that, when Julie emailed me, it went into my spam folder and it was only as I was deleting the spams that I noticed the name of Julie Cooke. She had written to say that she thought that I may be her husband's cousin.

When they came to visit us, I went to pick them up from a local hotel and as soon as they came out of the building, I knew it was Charlie as he was a complete ringer for my Dad. Spooky or what!!!

Of course, one thing that I remember to this day is Mother pulling out her hankie, (which I assume was clean but don't bank on that) and spitting on it and then using the said, now wet, hankie to rub clean your face and remove any grubby marks. This was usually done when visiting someone like a doctor or dentist, for good hygiene reasons !!!!! After all she did not want us to be seen as unhygienic or grubby in any way. Was this just our family or did other mothers do it? I sometimes wonder if certain traits were indicative of London or if those habits went on around the country.

My paternal grandparents were thespians and travelled throughout the country, which at that time included Ireland. That was where my paternal grandparents met and where some of their children were born. One of the biggest problems for a transient family at that time is that they often did not register the birth, for a variety of reasons, which could include apathy or just the ability or money to get on a bus and travel many miles to register the new child.

My grandparents obviously did not see that as a problem. At least two or possibly three of their children were never registered and as my mother and father were not married, it did not present itself as a problem. As my father came to England prior to independence, he did not need a passport and the only time that he ever went abroad was during the war when he went to Italy and they did not need a passport then!!

We think my father was born in Cork and although I spent some time going through the records in Cork, could find no trace of my father's birth. I also checked the records at Somerset House and alas, there was no trace there either.

As travelling thespians, they could not take a child with them wherever they went so very often they found families who would take them in. They may or may not have been kind people or they may have had extreme views, which they then passed on to the children that lived with them. But as far as two of the siblings were concerned, they were ok although not the most loving of people.

At this point in the book you must have noticed that our family has had a very colourful past and this must have come from my paternal grandparents, who were a little unorthodox to state the obvious.

When My Dad's brother Dermot was born, his parents were on tour and after a few months arrived in Ramsgate in Kent. They met a couple who had no children so they gave them the baby, not for adoption you understand and not for good, but like a modern-day footballer Dermot, was sent out "on loan". Yes, it does sound a bit weird now and it may have then, but that is the sort of family they were. It was not that they did not care, they did, and used to visit Ramsgate from time to time when in the area. Dermot's older brother Ken (who was brought up in Bangor in Northern Ireland) used to visit and take photographs for the rest of the family. Dermot stayed with that family until he joined the Army in WW2.

My paternal grandmother was Irish and her father was an officer in the Irish Army and would have been around 1890, many years before independence. My father was born in 1902 (we think) and knew all the Irish rebel songs and often could be heard approaching our flats singing "Kevin Barry" at the top of his very powerful voice.

My grandparents both lived very long lives, as did most of their children except for my Dad who died in 1958 aged 56. We must assume that was correct as it says aged fifty-six on his death certificate. But then again, it was my Mum who gave the information about his age, which my Father had told her, but he had been known to tell a few porkies in his life and he could have been older.

But he did not want to put my mother off, so he may have slashed a few years off his age, who knows, and that may have been the reason I could find no trace of his birth in 1902 in either England or Ireland. I also looked for any information about five years either side of that date.

As far as we know my Father was 13 years older than my Mother and another weird coincidence is that Dad died in 1958 aged 56 and mum died 13 years later in 1971 aged 56, spooky or what!!!

Dad also fell out with both his Father and all his brothers. Thanks to his brother Ken's detective skills, he told us that they had not spoken for many years, but none of us knew why, although I am sure that some have their suspicions. My Father's brother Dermot told his son that he had seen and spoken to my Father in Italy during the war but as far as I know they did not keep in touch after the war. All a bit weird I know.

I can tell you though that, as each of us approached our fifty-seventh birthday, we had a party to celebrate passing the tragic fifty-six !!!

Our upbringing did have some hints of violence as some of the previous pages have shown, but some we manufactured ourselves with a little help from guns (air rifles) and knives. Some use of guns was very good for example, when Albert shot rabbits and for the cooking pot.

Sometimes using guns was not so good, such as the time when my brother Bud was showing off his new air pistol. The lady from the upstairs flat, Maureen, was sat on our settee when Bud was pretending he was going to shoot her (wait for it) and when he pulled the trigger, guess what, yes you are right, there was a pellet up the spout. It hit Maureen on the arm, which started to swell immediately. When the old man got home, much to Bud's horror, he took the new air pistol off him and got rid of it. I think that's why he joined the army, to get his hands on bigger and better guns.

Bud was the smooth, cool one in the family. He would buy good quality shirts as soon as he started work and could afford them and he was always on the lookout for other things to buy. On one occasion, he decided to buy a motor bike.

Now this came as a bit of a surprise to everyone as Bud did not have a driving licence and had never driven a motor bike. Albert went with him to buy the motor bike but as neither of them had a licence and neither of them had a clue on how to ride the bloody thing, they pushed it all the way home, with the occasional ride on it when they were in quiet streets where there were no coppers.

The conclusion of this saga was that neither of them got a licence and after some time Bud thinks that he gave the motor bike to Brian our cousin.

Another of Bud's "buys" was a car, yes you are right. He still did not have a licence but I am not sure if he intended to get a licence or if he bought it to sell on and make a few bob. The car was a Lanchester and it was parked outside the flats for months and my mates and I used to play in it. One day we would be fighter pilots and the next day we would be racing drivers. It was great fun and of course, it was somewhere comfy to sit if it was pouring down with rain, but only if Bud was at work!

I think that Bud tried to sell the car but that did not work so in the end he thinks he either sold it or gave it away for scrap, but that was the end of our fighter pilot days.

We also had knives. In those days, most young lads had a knife which we used for all sorts of legal tasks. We did not have the need to go around stabbing other people, apart from family of course, and most young teenagers would have either a large penknife or even a sheath knife on their person most of the time, but of course they would not get away with that today.

One day, my brother Terry and I were playing in the garden just prior to Sunday lunch. We were playing a game where we placed the sheath knife upright in the ground and we each took equal paces away from the knife and when one of us said go, we would both dive and try to get the knife before the other. It was all going very well until I managed to get there first and got my hand firmly round the handle, but not firmly enough, as Terry managed to bash the top of my wrist made my fingers slide effortlessly down the blade, causing an awful lot of blood and a fair amount of tears; yes, both my blood and my tears.

I had to get on a bus by myself to the hospital, which was a fair old bus ride away. I am not sure how keen the bus conductor was to have this young lad bleeding all over his bus. I had a few stitches put in my fingers, which was both good and bad news. Firstly, the bad news is that by the time we had got home, there was a very small dinner saved for me and because I had trouble using my right hand, I swear that half my dinner was nicked. But out of adversity and all that, came the good news! Because I am right handed therefore I could not use that hand write, it was a waste of time going to school until the stitches had been removed. Yes, result!

I did not see school as anything other than an irritant that had to be avoided at all costs and some days I would try to think up elaborate schemes to avoid going. I would have the normal "tummy" pains but most mums knew that one so it did not work often. It only worked if it was coupled with the runs or chronic vomiting.

I would get 'pains' in the legs, arms, back, head and feet, bearing in mind, as I have said earlier, I was always ill as a child. So, if I said something was wrong they were inclined to err on the side of caution and that my friend, was my secret weapon!

Now who remembers crystal sets? I cannot remember all the details and I am not sure how we got the required bits or for that matter the instructions on how to do it, but I do know that with very few bits we made these sets which could pick up radio stations and in particular, Radio Luxemburg.

In those days, we did not have any state or commercial stations in this country which played pop music all the time. There were short programmes on the BBC, and Radio 1 had not started nor had the pirate radio stations such as radio Caroline. So, the BBC decided what you could listen to and if they wanted to ban a song such as "Tell Laura I love her" they could and did.

I remember going to a friend's house in the lunch break to listen to that song and, as he only lived on Downham Way just a few minutes from the school and his brother had bought the record. Luckily nobody missed us because we were not allowed out of school at break times without permission.

We would make our crystal sets and try to pick up Radio Luxemburg which did not start broadcasting until about 7pm and as the signal was not great, it would fade in and out. This was not helped by the fact that we would hide under the blankets to listen as we were supposed to be going to sleep. It was many years later when I was in the army and a mate of mine wanted to listen to the last song on radio Luxemburg. So, a few of us stayed up and listened to that last song which was called "At the end of the day" and I know the words still to this day. But I am not sure if Radio Luxemburg still exists and if it does, I wonder if it still plays that same song. I doubt it.

We did lots of sneaky things in or around the house so that Mum or Dad could not see us or catch us getting up to mischief. One place where we often went was to the toilet out on the balcony and it was there that my brother

Bud went to have a fag. Unfortunately for Bud, Dad wanted to go to the toilet. I don't think that we had a lock on the toilet door so when Dad threw open the door, they both got a shock - Dad to see Bud smoking and Bud to see he had been caught by his father, who immediately gave him a wallop around the head! The window of the toilet was closed so nobody knew where the fag went, and for years after and to this day, everyone believed that he swallowed the fag when Dad hit him!

That was not the only time that smoking got Bud into trouble. He was hanging around with a few mates on the bridge that goes over the railway line (it is still there) when he asked his mate for a fag. His mate started to tease him and in the end said that if you want the fag then go and threw it onto the line. Bud jumped the fence to get it just as the police arrived and in those days, they did not mess around. Bud was arrested for trespassing and went to court where he was fined. As far as I am aware he managed to never get into trouble with the police again, although he still managed to get up to more mischief.

Bud had been shopping for Mum and was carrying home two very heavy shopping bags when he saw a bike against a wall. As nobody locked up their bikes in those days (we never thought to do that), he decided that it was the quickest and easiest way to get home so he took the bike. He soon realised that Mother would go loopy if she thought he had stolen a bike, so when he got near to home, he put the bike under a bush and carried the shopping home. He told my eldest brother that on the way home he had seen a bike under a bush so they then went to see if it was still there. It was and after shouting at some younger kids who were also looking at the bike, my brother Albert said it was a decent bike and it looked as though it had been dumped!!! Yes ok, so you now know the truth!

They took the bike home, cleaned it up and painted it and Bud used it for some time. He also used it when he went scrumping and one day he put the bike against a fence and used it as a prop to get over the fence to nick apples. On his return with a jumper full of apples he discovered someone had stolen his bike. He was furious that anyone could stoop so low as to steal a bike! Wow, but all in all justice had been achieved.

When Bud left school, he worked in the same factory where many of the family worked from time to time. Bud was very keen on motorbikes and our cousin Brian, who worked at the same factory and also had a motorbike, so he offered to pick up Bud on a daily basis, but Bud was very often late. Brian would not be happy so on this occasion when Bud was late getting downstairs, he jumped on the back of the motorbike and before he could get himself secure, Brian opened the throttle and flew off down the road. Unfortunately, Bud also flew off down the road but he went backwards as Brian went forwards, but luckily Bud was not hurt.

Life was tough for my Mother. She had five children of her own and loads of other people staying in the flat.

There was no privacy and just the one toilet and sink and she was always worried about money or should I say, the lack of money. I am sure that there were days when she just wanted a little peace and quiet, to be able to sit on her own and have a cup of tea in front of the radio with no kids shouting and screaming around her.

One day when we were all playing in the street Mum opened the living room window to shout down that she and Maureen, from upstairs, were locked in the flat and could not get out. They lowered a basket down on a length of string with some money and a note to go to the shops and get some stale cakes and a packet of 10 fags. Of course, you could not do that today as they would not serve fags to a child. When we got back they lowered the basket for us to put in the required goods and they duly pulled it up again. It was only many years later that I realised that we had Yale locks on the front door and all they had done was put the latch up so we could not turn the key to unlock it.

Do remember that in those days we all had open fires. Some of the more "posh" people may have had a gas fire but none of our friends or relatives. We used logs, coal or even coke and for that matter we even used paper. Yes my mother would spread out a newspaper and then fold it in about 2 inch strips diagonally and then do a sort of criss cross pattern with the paper to make a small solid piece of paper that burnt a bit like a log. Ok, so it would not last long but at least it was some warmth and in fact we would throw anything on to the fire that would provide at least a little heat. Do remember that the dustman used to collect all and any rubbish and that included old tables, chairs or other bits of furniture, which they would take and sell them to the second-hand shop.

Sometimes on the way home we would see old furniture that had been left out for the dustmen and if we could carry it, we would take it home to burn on the fire. If we could not carry it, we would go home and get the pram and then use that to get the wood home. Don't forget that there was an awful lot of people doing the same thing so you had to be a bit nifty (fast) on your feet or you would leave one of the kids there to guard it while you went for the pram.

With the masses burning all sorts of rubbish, it should come as no surprise that London was full of smog for most of the winter. So much so that when I joined the Army my nickname was Smokey, because I came from the smoke e.g. London.

It was terrible, thick, black smog that got into your lungs and made you cough. The bus conductor would have to get off the bus and walk in front with a torch so that the driver could see where he was going and even the shortest trip seemed to take ages. Remember that you could not see very much at all further than about 3 or 4 feet in front of you in the smog so when we were up to mischief the local copper could not see us, although he would often shout out that he knew who we were !!! Mother would not stop worrying until we were all safely in the house.

This of course did have a number of positive sides to it as well. because if the conductor was walking in front of the bus, he was not available to collect the fares and as the old buses had open backs we could jump on or jump off at will.

Even if the weather was not bad we could get on the bus and saw that the conductor was upstairs as you could see him in an angled mirror at the top of the stairs. So as he came down the aisle towards the stairs, we would then jump off the bus without paying!!! I think it was in late in 1957 that there was a huge train crash at a place called St Johns, Lewisham in South London, when 90 people were killed and 173 were injured. It was on a day when the fog was particularly bad and happened during the rush hour on the 17.18pm from London. The only way to find out what was happening was to listen to the radio for updates but in those days they felt that if they gave you to much information it would affect morale and the infrastructure of society would collapse and there would be anarchy. So, there was not a lot of up to date news and what there was had come from the local station where people were gathered to try to find out any information on their loved ones.

We had a neighbour who sometimes caught that train home and there were others who also had loved ones on the train, but as luck would have it, our neighbour had been delayed and missed the train and nobody that we knew lost their lives. But ten years later there was another local rail crash at Hither Green but by that time I had joined the Army and left the area.

Chapter Nine - Leaving School & Various Jobs

Life was very straightforward in the 50's and early 60's, if you had the money you bought food or other essentials and if you did not have the money, then you went without. Easy really. As I said earlier, in those days we used to have the front door key on a piece of string hanging inside the letter box and we never got burgled. This is not strictly true as you will have already read that Mum chased a burglar around the streets with a carving knife in her hand, But in the main this did not happen because there were "*families*" that looked after many areas of London; names such as the Kray's or the Richardson's and many others. There were some things that you did not do, such as, you never robbed anyone worse off than yourself and, etched in stone was, you never shit on your own doorstep, which means you do not rob people who live near you. How very quant some of our sayings were!

Unfortunately, the old lady downstairs from us in the flats got robbed while she was out. Yes, they used the key on the length of string inside her letterbox and took many of her meagre possessions.

I remember Mum telling all the neighbours what had happened and the old lady received loads of support from many people but the surprise came a few days later when a van pulled up outside the flats and it was full of household items that the old lady had lost in the break in.

A few days later there was a rumour that a local thief was in hospital with two broken legs. Ah, that was when justice was seen to be done and no police or courts were involved, no long periods on bail or slippery solicitors trying to get you off to avoid justice. It was quick, efficient, cheap and was seen and appreciated by the locals. If you did abide by the rules then you would get supported by the "*Families*".

I left school in 1962 aged fifteen, which was the school leaving age, although to be honest I had not been to school much in the last year. As soon as I turned fifteen in mid-November I left, even though officially I could not leave until the end of the term, which was just before Christmas.

It was around this time that my brother Albert and his wife were offered a council house not far from where we lived. I am sure you can imagine their delight in being offered a house rather than a flat and the fact that it was not on a council housing estate, but in a private road.

After being allocated this house they had to buy furniture etc. and have it delivered but as they both worked full time they asked me to go to the house where the only bit of furniture was a hard chair. That was one of the coldest winters on record, but they were very caring and gave me a one bar electric fire to try and keep warm. It was bloody freezing and I would have been warmer waiting in the morgue, but the furniture did come eventually and I was able to leave the house (I swear it was bloody warmer outside) and walk home.

I did go into school on the last day but to be frank, it was a total waste of time. In those days if you were not bright enough to gain formal qualifications you would receive a school leaving certificate, which was supposed to prove that you attended school and attained at least a basic understanding of reading, writing and arithmetic. Unfortunately, due to my rather erratic school attendance, they refused to give me a school leaving certificate and as far as I was aware, I was the only pupil in my year to get absolutely bloody nothing. I did not take any exams so did not get anything there. As I said, they did not give me a school leaving certificate, although I had a suspicion it gave the headmaster some form of satisfaction or joy, bless him.

I only went into school on that last day to say goodbye to my friends so I did not care and as we left the school on that last day my headmaster was at the gate. He very kindly informed me that I was so thick I would not even be able to get a job as a dustman. As it happened, my Uncle Len was a dustman and did very well thank you. He not only got well paid but they also had several little scams that kept the wolves away from the door or in other words, they managed to eat well and pay all the bills.

I just smiled as I did not have the heart to tell him that I already had a job to start the day after Boxing Day. Wow !!! And the fact that I had been working most of the time for the past year when I should have been in school, so getting a job was not any problem at all.

On Boxing Day morning I was getting my stuff ready for my first day at my first job the following day in an engineering factory about 3 or 4 miles away. It did not take long on the bus or train to get there. By lunchtime it had started to snow and it continued snowing all day and all night and all week, and in fact it, snowed on and off for the next couple of months. There were still clumps of snow on the side of the railway lines in late May and early June 1963.

I went to the train station the next morning but there were no trains. I waited for a bus but there were no buses, so in the end I decided to walk and arrived at my fist day of my first ever full time proper job over an hour late. But at least I had made it, unlike most of the other workers, but I was freezing bloody cold and covered in snow. I must have looked like nothing on earth, although I suppose I could have been used to scare the local kids.

But the bosses were at least good enough to let us knock off early so the we could get home at a reasonable hour. Some of the workers had walked for about 2 hours just to get to work. I don't think that would happen in these days, do you?

I could tell many stories about my very brief time working in that factory, but there is one story that I must tell. Remember that I was just 15 and looked about 12 with very little experience of both life in general and women. When I began working in the factory most of the other machine operators were older women and they took immense pleasure in winding up both myself and another young lad, who had started working there at the same time.

Most of their banter would be sexual and they would try and mainly succeed, in embarrassing us with their remarks. After a couple of weeks of this, we decided that the time was right for revenge. The main protagonist was an older woman, who after arriving at work every day, had an routine to get ready to start on her machine. She would hang up her handbag, then take off and hang up her coat, put on her apron, kick off her shoes and slip into her comfortable slippers.

Only this day we had both got into work early and nailed her slippers to the floor! Now keep this image in your head - she kicked off her shoes, slipped into her slippers and then as she tried to walk away, fell arse over head! What a great result, with everyone else thinking it was very funny. She spent the rest of the day trying to kill us and luckily by the next day she could see the funny side of it.

I only worked in that factory for a matter of weeks before deciding that factory work was not for me, Mother always said that you should look for and get another job before giving in your notice. Don't forget that in the early 60's there were loads of jobs available for young people and if you looked in either the Evening Standard or the Evening News there was page after page of "junior vacancies".

I decided that I fancied working in one of the world's poshest hotels, which for a kid from a council estate seemed to be aiming very high. I went for an interview at the Savoy Hotel in London for the job of as a "Page Boy", as I fancied wearing one of those fancy hats, but alas I did not get the job as they said I was too tall. However, the experience of going into a "posh" hotel made me want to work in one even more, so I applied to the Piccadilly Hotel as a "Page Boy" and I was successful and got the job.

That job was good for me as I learnt that you did not have to pay out for decent clothes because you could go to work in any old gear, put on a uniform and look very smart during your shift. At the end of the day you changed back into your normal clothes and went home.

In my time at the Piccadilly Hotel I saw and met some very famous people such as the Duke of Edinburgh, Cassius Clay, later to become Mohammed Ali, Arthur Hains and many other T.V. stars of that era.

Now do remember that as a working-class lad from a council estate I never thought for one moment that I would ever see a celebrity or royalty in the flesh, let alone talk to them but in the Piccadilly hotel I would see them every day. When I went home and told the family that I had met some well-known TV personality, I am sure that they thought that I was making it up.

When Cassius Clay stayed at the hotel life was rather hectic, as he had a large entourage and of course his manager Angelo Dundee, who just before the fight bet me 2/- that Henry Cooper would lose to Cassius. Do remember that as a young South Londoner Henry Cooper was my idol and he was also a national hero.

Henry managed to flatten Cassius in the fight but he was saved by the bell and then of course it was delayed further because Cassius had a cut on his glove (bloody convenient). That in fact turned the fight round and it was stopped because Henry had a terrible cut above his eye.

At a function the day or two after the fight I was on cloakroom duties when Angelo Dundee came over. I thought that he had come over to claim his 2/- but he then told me that if it was not for the bell and the split glove, it would have been a knockout so he would not take my money and, in fact gave me 10/-! Wow what a nice man!

Another nice man was a very popular and much loved T.V. comedian at that time and his name was Arthur Hains. On one particular occasion, I had to go up Regent Street to an airline office to collect some tickets and he said that he would walk with me. When I came out of the airline office he was still there and said that as he had time to kill so he thought that he would wait for me and walk back to the hotel with me. What a nice man he was and to tell the truth, I felt a bit like a T.V. star myself as people were staring and looking at us! It made my week!

I had some great times working at that hotel and it helped me no end in building my confidence and self-esteem. I was popular with most of the other staff except one!! The Head Hall Porter was a horrible man, full of his own self-importance and for some reason, he did not like me one bit. To be honest I am not sure that he liked anyone but himself, as all the hall porters used to moan about him as they felt that he often kept tips that were meant for them. He also did that to us but very often we were unaware of it.

One day when I was on my way up the staff stairs after lunch, he was waiting for me. He said, "Do you like me young Cooke?" and as I am sure you realise by now my gob seems to start working before the brain is in gear, I said "No sir, I do not like you" Well, he seemed very impressed and said how he admired people who told the truth and a few days later he sacked me!!!

I was half expecting it so I was not surprised, but I had seen an advert for a Page Boy at the Strand Palace Hotel and when I went along for an interview with the Head Porter he asked me if the Head Porter at the Piccadilly Hotel had asked me if I liked him. Wow, how the bloody hell did he know that? But he then told me that many years previously he used to work for the same bloke and he was asked the same question and also answered *No*. He too was sacked. He then gave me the job and I got on very well with him.

For a period of just over two years I had loads of jobs, trying to find my niche in life. I got a job as a van boy for a removal firm and, bearing in mind that I was a very weak and skinny kid, don't ask me how I got that job. There were two van boys and the other lad was bloody huge.

He was not very bright but he could lift heavy things and because the other lad had given in his notice to join the Army, I was told that I had got the job. But he then changed his mind and I thought I would get the chop but the owner said that was not fair on me so he kept us both on.

At one point, I felt that I would make a great car salesman (well I thought that I had the gift of the gab!) and the job sounded right up my street. So, I applied for a job at a second-hand car sales in Catford and got the job. When I turned up five minutes early the other salesman said we should nip out for an early fag, but the boss saw us and said that it did not matter if I was early, if I was on site then I should be working. So I told him to stuff his job and left the building. As I left and walked up the road the town hall clock struck nine, so in effect I had in fact left a job before I had even started, not bad eh!

Another job which had a funny start but which I did manage to stay at for about six months was as a labourer for a scaffold company. The first day's job was to take down some scaffolding around an incinerator chimney at Lewisham Hospital. As the new labourer, I was not allowed on to the scaffold but the workmen threw down the scaffold poles and as they descended, my job was to collect them and make a neat pile ready to be put on to the lorry. I had not been doing it for long when one of the scaffolders fell and hit the deck very hard and the Forman was shouting from the top of the scaffolding "don't let him move, hold him down".

Bearing in mind that I was a rather skinny and weak sixteen-year-old, it was not an easy task but the good thing about the whole affair was that the accident investigators had to come and inspect the scaffold. We spent most of the day in a local café, another result, and fortunately the bloke was not seriously hurt and came out of hospital the next day.

Every job that we got on the scaffolding was allocated an amount of time. It may be a day or a week but if you got the job finished sooner and then went on to the next job, you would get paid the extra days.

We had a job given to us which was not really in our area but as there were no other gangs available, we had to do it. We had to take down a huge amount of scaffolding that went right along the length of a school and two stories high. When we got on site we found that the scaffolding was the new alloy poles which were so much lighter than the old steel poles and a lot easier to put up and take down, but our ganger saw a new way of working by sitting four of us on the flat roof, undoing the retaining ties and pushing with our legs so that the whole bloody lot came down in one big heap. We then spent a couple of hours undoing the fixings and stacking the poles ready for collection and it was all finished by lunch time. Not bad for a job that was supposed to take us three days, and of course we ended up getting two extra day's pay.

Everyone kept telling me that I had the gift of the gab or in other words, I was a gobby little geezer. So, when I saw an advert for a door to door salesman, selling vacuum cleaners, I thought wow, this could be the job for me but how wrong could you be?

I would end up telling an old lady that if I was in her shoes, I would not buy a new vacuum cleaner from a bloke on her doorstep.

My father was a funny sort of bloke. I cannot remember an awful lot about him but every now and then small things happen which remind me of him or of his idiosyncrasies.

My father was a great wordsmith. Everyone said he must have kissed the blarney stone (and yes, both myself and my younger son Glenn have kissed the blarney stone) and he could talk himself out of most trouble. He also enjoyed writing poetry, short funny skits and lyrics for songs. He knew the lady who wrote "Messing about on the river" and a man called Paul Fenlaway, who I believe conducted the BBC light orchestra.

Some years after he died I saw many of his works and I still remember one to this day.

"Fish and chips, fish and chips

That's the grub to feed them
Fish for brains
Chips for brawn
That's for the men who need them.
The parson in his sermon said
When dealing with your quips,
The only thing to put you right
Is a plate of fish and chips."

There were many more verses to that prose but I only remember those two. I remember there being hundreds of pages of writing and it is a shame that they were lost or destroyed, and now as I am getting (a little) older and have more time, I would have loved going through all his ramblings and maybe even added to them. That would have been fun!!

We once went up to Chesterfield on what was called a holiday. It was all a bit strange and made worse by the fact that I only remember some of it. It has since been said that we were there because the old man was running away after nicking the takings from the ice cream firm.

Mum, Dad, Bubs and myself all stayed with the vicar in the vicarage but my two older brothers were billeted in a boarding school just up the road and as it was in the school holidays, there was plenty of bed space. I would be sent up the road to get my brothers in the mornings and they would come back to the vicarage for their breakfast. On the morning of our last full day, I went up as usual to get my brothers and on the way back to the vicarage we were walking on top of a twelve-foot-high wall. At this point one of my loving brothers gave me a hefty shove and over the bloody wall I went, landing on my head, (ok, I have heard all the jokes and little sarcastic comments).

I spent a large part of the day being sick and in the end, they took me to the local hospital where they said that I had concussion and they would have to keep me in hospital under observation for another day or two. This upset the family plans a bit as we were all going home the next day, so in the end my Dad stayed behind while the rest of the family went home and we followed a few days later. The funny thing is I do not remember anything about being sick or being admitted to hospital or even coming home afterwards and yet I can still remember the layout of the lounge in the vicarage.

The main thing that I remember about Chesterfield was the church spire, which was crooked and known as the Crooked Spire.

That trip was the only time I remember going anywhere as a child apart from the day out each year at the Admiralty sports day.

I cannot recall going anywhere with Mum and Dad but when I was a bit older, about twelve I remember going with my eldest brother and his wife, Albert and Jean and their children to Allhallows on the isle of Grain in Kent. You had to change trains onto a steam train that went to Allhallows and in those days, it was a big adventure, as was a day out to Leysdown on the Isle of Sheppey, which was a little more commercialised than Allhallows and even had a few amusements for the children.

It was on a trip to Leysdown that my sister said, "Who farted" and we all got a little miffed as none of us admitted it but we then realised that she was reciting the name of a boat called "*Hoof Hearted*"!

On one occasion when the family went to Allhallows, I was not with them. They were on the train returning home when my nephew, who was a baby at the time, and was sitting on my mother's lap started to have a very nasty convulsion. They pulled the emergency cord and as far as I have been told, the train stopped and the guard came to the carriage to see what the emergency was, bearing in mind that the trains were made up of individual carriages with no corridor connection. So, when they realised that it was a very real emergency, the train sped to the next station where there was an ambulance waiting to whisk the baby off to the nearest hospital. As it happens he never had another seizure in his life - strange how these things can come and then go.

Chapter Ten - Rhyming Slang, Sayings & Songs

I remember going swimming with Albert and his eldest son, and as far as I am aware it was Albert who taught me to swim. I cannot remember learning and it seems that I was always able to swim. I also remember another of Albert's sons, who used to love jumping in from either the side or from the diving board; the only problem was that he could not swim. So as soon as we all got changed into our swimming trunks, Albert would run into the pool area and then I understood why, he had to be there to jump in and pull his son out of the water.

I can't remember learning to ride a bike either, so I do not know if it was Albert who taught me that as well. To be honest, in those days we were a little more robust and we would just get on a bike and try and ride it. Yes, we would fall of a hundred times but by the time we went indoors for food, we would know how to ride a bike, although we were covered in cuts and bruises. I remember Albert would help us put together all the old bike bits to make a usable machine and today we would call it re-cycling. As I said earlier, it was Albert who took on the role of Man of the House when Dad died in 1958 and continued to do so right up until they got their own council house in about 1963.

Many years later when I was married and living in Essex, Albert and Jean came to stay for the week-end and my elder son asked Albert if he could repair his bike. After a couple of hours, I became aware that many of my son's friends were going down the drive at the side of our house and when I went to investigate, I found a line of young lads with their bikes waiting for Albert to repair them and he was loving it!!

One day my brother Bud said he could hear Albert running down the street towards our house and Bud said that he could tell it was Albert by the way he ran. Then he appeared in the road outside, flew into the flats at great speed, then flew up the stairs getting close to the speed of light; in through the front door and then !!**!! too late, he could hold it no longer. With only the slightest of coughs, it was seen running down his legs. Oh well, it was a good try and he very nearly made it and I am sure that nobody said anything about it!!!

If you needed to go for "big jobs" in a public toilet it used to cost you a penny. This in fact was very excellent value as there was an awful lot of graffiti written on the walls inside the cubicles. In the main this was the only place where you would see graffiti in those days and not on the side of people's houses or shop fronts.

To this day, I still remember one little ditty on the wall of the cubicle and it went:

"Here am I broken hearted, paid a penny and only farted"

Some wag had written underneath:

"Here am I crafty and artful, I paid a penny and shit a cart full"

Bud decided it was time for him to see the big wide world and to that end he decided to join the Army. I cannot remember his early days in the Army but I do remember he was posted to Middle Wallop with the Army Air Corps where he met his wife-to-be.

Marlene came from Doncaster and had a very funny accent, which most of us could not understand. She had also come from a poor background, as did most soldiers at that time, as joining the forces enabled you to escape the poverty.

They decided to get married in the Registry Office in Lewisham, South London on a Saturday morning and to hold the reception at our flat in the evening. But this presented a problem as the ladies were going to make up the buffet during the afternoon between the wedding and the reception. This meant that the men and boys were just hanging about getting in the way, so a family friend, Ken, came up with an idea that the men and boys all go to the maritime museum for the afternoon getting back in time to meet and greet in the early evening. As far as I remember, it was a good trip but remember that when we were younger we would often end up in the Maritime Museum if we were in Greenwich at the beach and it started raining. So, we all knew where to go and what to see. My brother Bud got married, then left his new wife making sandwiches while he went off with the lads! She should have realised then that he was *master of keeping out of the way* and he must be good at it as they have been married for over 50 years.

As far as I remember that was the first time we'd had a party of any kind in our flat and although we had been to parties at both Aunt Win's and Uncle Harry's, we did not have any, so I would think that Bud and Marlene paid for most or all of the food and drink.

I was only fifteen at that time and did not drink a lot, even when out with friends. The pubs in those days were not very particular about how old you were as long as you had the money to pay for the pint. If a policeman did put his head in the door, then you made sure that your pint was nearer to the person next to you, so the policeman would think it was his. So, to find free drink in our house at Bud and Marlene's wedding was like hitting the jackpot and I drank more whisky than I should have done and was very quickly getting rat faced (very drunk). My eldest brother, Albert substituted my glass of whisky for one of cold tea and much to the bloody amusement of the rest of the family, I did not even notice! This was made worse by Albert laying on the floor in front of me and telling *me* to get up off the floor! Oh, happy days!!!

Bud and Marlene had married quarters in a village called Ham in Wiltshire (yes, I know it sounds silly) and I used to go and visit them there. It was in the country and after growing up in smog filled London, it really was a breath of fresh air. Of course, I enjoyed going to the local pub and, although I was only sixteen or seventeen it was never a problem and to this day I still have very fond memories of Doris (I think that was her name) doing a very traditional Wiltshire broom dance.

There were so many sayings in London at that time that you are inclined to forget them, then you hear something that reminds you of them. For instance, my Mother would often call my sister *Fanny Fanackerpan*, no don't ask me why, but it was a saying that I have not heard for many years. My sister remembered it recently, and asked why would you call someone that name. Well, it was meant to imply that you were a proper little miss or you were trying to be "posh"!

Another word that we used and was in fact part of a Chas and Dave song many years later, was "*cowson*" and was probably used in place of a swear word beginning with B******. You would often hear adults refer to a young person as '*a rotten little cowson*'. It was a derogatory word but back in the 50's it was used an awful lot, or maybe it was just my family that used it an awful lot and maybe that was because we had a lot of little 'cowsons' as both friends and family.

We often threatened our friends with a "*bunch of fives*" or a "*Five finger sandwich*" both of which meant that we would punch them as both meant "a fist".

If my sister asked Mum for a drink she would say "what have we got" e.g. orange squash and Mum would reply "*Adams Ale*" and for those of you who have never heard this expression it meant tap water.

If we were going out or going to a specific place we would often ask how will we get there and the reply was nearly always "*Shank's Pony*" which meant you will have to walk!!

If you had been very busy and someone asked you how you were you may have said that you have been running around like a "*Blue Arsed Fly*" but now I am not aware if flies have blue arses.

As a Londoner when I speak I often drop my H's so for instance, that man (h)ad (h)eart trouble but he had a nice (h)ouse. If someone said look at that (h)orse, we would not say "*a* orse" but we would say "*an* orse". Now to get this in perspective remember dear old Shakespeare who wrote "Dick the Shit" (Richard the Turd) said *"anorse, anorse my kingdom for anorse"*!

We were not Cockneys, we were from South of the river but we still used a lot of rhyming slang and for that matter, I still use some today. When I get dodgy looks from my son's I have to explain what things mean. I was out with my younger son recently when a friend commented on my "cheesecutter" and I could tell by the look on my son's face that he did not have a clue what that meant. It was the word we always used for a flat cap, don't ask me why.

With rhyming slang, you do not use the whole saying, for instance you would just say "apples" instead of "apples and pears" for stairs, so, he went up (or fell down) the apples. Now I know this sounds a bit patronising, but I hope that there will be people reading this book who do not know or who have never heard of rhyming slang.

Dad was often Brahms (and Litz = pissed) and would sometimes need help along the Frog (and Toad = road) and up the Apples.
Words like Barnet (Fair = Hair), Mincers (Mince Pies = Eyes), take a Butchers (Hook = Look) or Boat (Race = Face) and there are many more that I use every day.

But because of that I do not think of them as anything unusual until someone asks what I am talking about. Some, such as a cup of Rosie Lee (Tea), Brown Bread (Dead), Syrup of Figs (Wigs) are still heard in many places outside of London where Londoners may have settled and passed on the sayings to their children and even grandchildren.

I now live by the sea in Kent where a lot of Londoners settled in the past and in fact many still retire to live by the sea. Very often you can hear the odd slang words still used every day and one friend, who owns pubs and comes from South London, still uses monetary slang.

Another way of talking so that others outside of your circle could not understand you was to use "Back Slang". This was very difficult to perfect and many people (including myself) were hopeless at it, but my brother Terry was very good and loved showing off to his friends and using it as much as possible to confuse us all.

The girls would all use various songs or ditties when skipping but the only one that I remember hearing (no, I did not do the bloody skipping) was -:

> *"Bobby Shaftoe went to sea*
> *Silver buckles on his knee*
> *He'll come home and marry me*
> *Bonny, Bobby Shaftoe."*

There was a TV show called Out of Town and their theme song went like this -:

"Say what you will the countryside is still" etc, etc.

But children and young people had a knack of making up their own words and with the help of my sister, we managed to put together nearly all the first verse but we were stuck on the last line or two. After using social media, we did get some outside help, so here goes -;

> *"Say what you will*
> *School dinners make you ill*
> *Davey Crocket died of shepherd's pie*
> *All school din dins*
> *Come from pig bins*
> *Out of town"*

Another song that we bastardised was Rule Britannia and it went like this-:

> *"Rule Britannia*
> *2 tanners make a bob*

3 make one and six
And 4 two bob."

I am sure that there were many other songs we put our own words to but those two seemed to stick in my mind, which is probably a reflection on the state of my mind.

Washing day was another "occasion" as everything was washed by hand in those days. The whites such as sheets, other bedding and towels were boiled in the boiler that we used for bathwater and every now and then it would be agitated by a large lump of wood operated by hand.

Everything else would be washed in the kitchen sink and this would also include babies and younger children. In the winter or if it was raining, the clothes would be hung out to dry on the balcony (but not the babies) and if the wind was in the wrong direction, it would blow the rain onto the clothes and they could take days to dry.

In the summer or warmer weather all washing would be hung on the line in the garden and sometimes the kids would either carry it down the stairs for Mum or help her bring it back up. But do remember that in those days we did not change our clothes every day. Mum would first inspect them for obvious dirt stains and if there were none, she would then smell them. So if there were no obvious stains and they did not smell, you could wear them for at least one more day and possibly even two! The same method applied to the food!!!

I think it was some sort of philosophy that you only cleaned anything if it started to look dirty or it started to smell. This was the same for floors, bedding, sinks, clothes, food and even kids. That is why we only had a bath once a week. If we had not had any of little accidents like wetting the bed, had a follow through (a wet fart) or were sick, then we would still not have another bath until Sunday, but we would have an extensive and extra strip wash using the kitchen sink. Life did not stop for you and even though you may have been naked in the kitchen with shit running down the side of your leg, anyone could still walk in or pass through on the way to the toilet. Unsurprisingly they would make some form of nasty or sarcastic comment!

After my Dad died in 1958 times got harder and Mum had a number of cleaning jobs (as I said earlier) on top of doing the rags and making chimney pots. One of her employers even asked her to marry him, though I suspect it may have had nothing to do with love, but quite a lot to do with Mum's ability to cook and clean!

If I had to phone her while she was at work, she would answer the phone in her posh voice. She could not keep this up for long, just long enough to say the telephone number and of course the customary, "Can I be of help?" but once she realised it was me, she would revert back to the "common" denominator with "Oh it's you, you silly sod". Yes, I always felt loved!

I left home to join the Army in 1965 and although we had moved to a house on the same estate, we still had no telephone, fridge, freezer or any kind of central heating. How times have changed, these days most eight-year olds have their own mobile phones, iPads or laptops.

One of the other perks of Mum's jobs was that the people she worked for would ask me to cut their lawns, for which I was paid a fair wage. Bear in mind that they both had petrol mowers (most people had the old hand held push mower, which was bloody hard work) which made life rather easy and I also enjoyed seeing how the other half lived.

Another part of our life were girlfriends. We all had special friends who were girls from a very early age, but I know that mine started with Pauline P, who was a lovely girl with a smashing Mum. When my Dad died, she was very kind to me but when we went to senior school we both went different ways, but that it not the end of the story.

About 10 years later when I was coming home on leave from the Army, I was on the train from Charing Cross in the rush hour and after we had been going for a few minutes a really nice looking young lady asked me if my name was Keith. Wow, I was shocked as I felt sure that I did not know her. When I said "Yes, it is", she then told me her name and yes, you are right, it was Pauline P!

Another of my young loves was a girl called Anita, who lived just off the Downham Way on Northover. She was a nice girl but her mother kept trying to get me to eat her home-made soup, which was called a milk soup and to be honest it was terrible. Even Anita would not eat it, aarrgghh

But again, we are at the point where every adult woman would see me as a poor little skinny thing that needed feeding up and they felt that they should supply me with extra food. The only good thing about that was that I would often take home food and other members of the family would gratefully eat it.

The Learning Curve - Aarh memories!

This is where you learn a little more about the use of some of our sayings and idiosyncrasies, which are still alive and well to this day. Many of the sayings are from London but some have gone from London to other parts of the country.

The South London accent has always sounded rather common and from me it still does! It seems to get worse when I mix with other Londoners and all the funny little sayings that follow can still be heard today, especially in my house.

DUCKING AND DIVING – This relates to finding ways to make money, get coal or get some form of food by, for example, scrumping (see below) sometimes legally, sometimes very close to illegal and of course the downright illegal.

SQUATTING IN A PROPERTY – During and after the war many people were made homeless so they would have to look for a habitable property and live there until the owner returned and threw them out. They did not pay rent but it did give them some respite from either the war or the wintry weather and of course they looked after the property. But had it stayed empty, it may have decayed a lot quicker and not been fit for habitation when the owners returned.

FAGS – unlike our American friends, this does not relate in any way to a person's sexuality. It is in fact a slang word for cigarettes and a **FAG END** (stop it!!!) is the cigarette end or butt, also sometimes referred to as a **DOG END,** but don't ask me why.

FAGGOTS – Here we go again; no, it is not what you may be thinking. Faggots are made from pigs' offal and they can still be bought, but they are frozen and I think many people are put off as they are packaged as **Mr BRAIN'S FAGGOTS** - many people think they are made from brains, but that's the manufacturer's name. I like them and eat them on a regular basis.

A GUZUNDER – back in the 50's and early 60's we did not have, and had never heard of, an *en-suite* toilet. Many houses and flats had outside toilets so in the very cold weather we had a bowl (sometimes called a potty) that "Guzunder" the bed for the night time pee. The worst part was having to empty it the following morning and you had to be very careful not to spill any, lovely!!

PISSED – this word has two meanings. The first meaning is you are if you are drunk, and if you are very pissed, then you are what is called **SHIT FACED, RAT FACED or RAT ARSED** or 'Pissed as a Newt' and please do not ask where they come from. But if you are **PISSED OFF** it means you are fed up or annoyed with someone or something.

PRE-DECIMAL MONEY – Prior to 1971 the currency in the UK was Pounds, Shillings and Pence, with 240d (that's pennies) to the Pound. The coins we had were a ½ crown, which was 2 shillings and six pence or 30d; a

2-shilling coin, known as a 2-bob coin or 24d; a 1 shilling coin or 12d; a sixpence known as a tanner or 6d; a 3 pence coin or 3d; a penny or 1d; a half penny or ½d and a farthing. There were 4 farthings to a penny. Now you can see why we went decimal.

SKINT – This meant, and still means, that you have no money and sometimes also referred to as **BRASSIC (LINT)** which is rhyming slang for **SKINT.**

SCRUMPING – I suppose it is just another word for stealing but specifically aimed at fruit such as apples, pears and plums. But it is the fruit which had fallen off the trees in windy weather and lay on the ground which became known as **WINDFALLS.** It was still stealing but a little more acceptable to the local copper and society.

DRIPPING – After you have cooked a joint of beef or pork there is a lot of fat left in the bottom of the baking tray, and if you pour this fat into a bowl and let it go cold, the jelly goes to the bottom and the fat stays on top. You should always mix the fat and the jelly before eating it and it is best on toast as the fat soaks in, ahh lovely!

WINKLES – Anyone not from London may not know what these are as I have not seen them a lot in the past few years. They are very small shells with the **WINKLE** inside and the only way to get it out is with a small pin and, although the taste is not unpleasant, you do need an awful lot to fill you up. Winkles were supplied by the winkle man, who would come around on his bike on Sunday afternoons, with a big basket on the front, selling all types of seafood such as shrimps, whelks, winkles and eels.

BUBBLE AND SQUEAK - This is mashed potato and cabbage, which has been cooked and then mixed together and then fried until they are golden brown and crispy. I am not sure if anyone makes it any more, as it is still cheap to buy in the supermarkets. The Irish side of the family call it Colcannon.

STUFFED HEARTS – These are Lambs or Pigs hearts that are cleaned up and stuffed with sage and onion, or other stuffing depending on taste. We used to eat them on a regular basis. You can still buy them but most of the younger generation would not even try them.

PIGS TROTTERS – These are pigs' feet, you see, they sound delicious straight away! They were boiled until very soft and well cooked and were often served with either peas or yellow peas pudding or of course onions. You don't seem to see them today but pigs still have feet so what happens to the pigs' trotters? Do they go into other pork products such as pork sausages, I wonder?

RAG AND BONE MAN – He would come around on the same day every week and you would get your china from him in return for any old rags. He had a horse and cart and still used a horse up until I left home to join the Army. He would come around in all weathers, rain or shine.

GROUNDED – This meant the same as it does today, however, we would be told that we were 'grounded' for the week but after a couple of days, our parents would be so fed up with having us around the house that they would give in and let us go out.

CLIP ROUND THE EAR – Very often if the local policeman caught you doing something that was a minor infringement of the law, he would either tell you off or **CLIP** you round the ear. Of course, all parents knew this so if you arrived home with a very red ear they would immediately assume that you had been breaking the law. We had to lie and say that we had been play fighting with our mate or they would give you a **CLIP** round the other ear too!!

POKER – This did not refer to the card game but to the long round piece of solid steel that adults would use to poke the fire to keep it going. Or in the case of our family, it would often be thrown at the kids if they were misbehaving in any way or being cheeky to Mother. The sad thing is that we did not see this as odd in any way and thought that it was quite normal, as did our friends.

HOPPING THE WAG – Now I have no idea of the origin of this saying but we all used it, children and adults, and it meant an unauthorised absence from school. Sometimes children would be hopping the wag when their parents thought they were at school.

THE ODDFELLOWS – This was a sort of social and friendship club open to anyone to join. They have been in existence since 1810, so just a bit older than myself. They have many roles including helping those most in need, which they did with us and they continue to carry out this role even today, over 200 years since it started.

CHAISE LOUNGE – They were very common in those days and best described as a Sofa or Couch with an arm at one end and nothing at the other end so you could sleep on it if you so desired. Of course, today a Victorian Chaise Longe would be much sought after and very expensive to buy.

NATIONAL ASSISTANCE OFFICE – I suppose today it would be known as the Social Security Office but in those days, you would only get any money if you were in dire need e.g. to feed the children and of course, it only lasted a very short period of time.

GAS AND ELECTRIC METER REBATES – You paid for your gas and electric by putting coins into a meter and when the meter reader emptied the meter, they would take the reading and tell you how much you owed. They would take out all the foreign coins and count the rest. They would then take out the money that was owed and anything left was called a rebate which was yours. Of course, sometimes that rebate would mean decent food on the table for the next couple of days.

TOMMY GUN – A sub machine gun called a Thomson, was used both during and after the war. Many households had weapons from the war years and it was not seen as a big deal.

A CLOUT – Now for a non-Londoner this could be rather confusing, as there are two interpretations for this word. The first refers to a clout e.g. someone hitting you such as a "clout" round the head and the second interpretation is a little bit more delicate as it was slang for a lady's vagina. So, if asked if you want a clout, this could confuse young lads.

THE TALLY MAN – Most working class people in the 50's and early 60's could not afford to go out and buy all sorts of things for the house such as new sheets, blankets curtains or suites, so the way that they managed was to buy them from the Tally Man. He would come around with his van every week and sell you what you needed but you did not have to pay for them then. He would come to your door each week and collect the money until the goods had been paid for and he would try to sell you more for just a couple of shillings extra each week.

MONETARY SLANG – This means using terms to describe amounts of money that others may not know such as a Pony which is £25, or a Monkey which is £500. A lot of people still use those terms today even though they may not be Londoners or live in London.

A WET FART – This would be if you thought that you had a bit of flatulence and farted (passed wind) but in fact you had a dose of diarrhoea, so what came out was not wind but a rather runny and smelly shit!!

The End Is Nigh!!

So, we come to the end of that part of my life and it is only when writing this book that I realised what a very colourful family we had! From thespians to lay preachers but for most adults, it was a very hard existence where each day brought yet another problem that had to be overcome. Yes, they did overcome the hurdles that life threw at them and for the most part we all grew up to be fairly normal people. Ok, ok I did say 'fairly' normal!

Many of the people mentioned in this book are still alive so the very hard, early years must have helped their resilience. The foods were healthy as most of it was fresh and was either very local or from some other part of the UK and not from the other side of the world. There were one or two exceptions, for example bananas, which we did not often see and when we did see them they were a bit on the expensive side.

The children seemed a lot happier then but our expectations were a lot lower. Today's children feel deprived if the do not have the latest iPad, iPhone or games console and we would have been delighted to get a new football for our birthday or Christmas present.

Printed in Great Britain
by Amazon